WENSL

in the NORTH RI

Mallerstang
To Kirkby
Stephen

Hell Gill

Ure Head

Cotterdale

Hearne Beck

Great Shunnor Fell

The Buttertubs Pass

To Muker To R

Shaw Paddock

Lunds

Old Road

Abbotside

Moorcock Inn

Hawes Junction

Nossdale

Fossdale

Stags Fell

Skellgill

Garsdale
to Sedbergh and
The Lake District

Appersett

Hardraw Sedbusk

ASH

Widdale Fell

Widdale

Sleddale

HAWES

Gayle Butterset

Wether Fell

Roman Road

Carr End

Countersett

Crag

Marsett

BAINBRIDGE

Addlebro

Carp

SEMERWATER
Stalling Busk

St
Fe

Old road
to Dentdale

Snaizeholme

High Houses

Dodd Fell

Bardale

Raydale

Cragdale

Newby Head

To Dentdale

Cam Houses

Kids
Pass

To Ribblehead
and Ingleton

To Oughtershaw
and Wharfedale

To Bucka

Buckden P

Langstrothdale

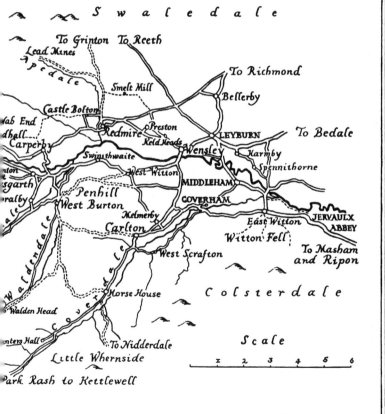

EYDALE

NG *of* YORKSHIRE

S w a l e d a l e

To Grinton   To Reeth

Lead Mines

To Richmond

Smelt Mill

Bellerby

Castle Bolton

ab End
dhall
Carperby

Redmire   Preston

Keld Heads

LEYBURN

To Bedale

Swinithwaite

Wensley

Harmby

West Witton

Spennithorne

garth
ralby

Penhill

MIDDLEHAM

West Burton

COVERHAM

Melmerby

JERVAULX
ABBEY

Carlton

East Witton

Witton Fell

To Masham
and Ripon

West Scrafton

C o l s t e r d a l e

Horse House

Walden Head

To Nidderdale

Scale

nters Hall

Little Whernside

1   2   3   4   5   6

Park Rash to Kettlewell

Marie Hartley

WENSLEYDALE

Hawes

WENSLEYDALE

BY

ELLA PONTEFRACT

in collaboration with and
with wood-engravings by

MARIE HARTLEY

SMITH SETTLE

First published in 1936 by
J. M. Dent & Sons Ltd

This edition published in 1988 by

Smith Settle Ltd
Ilkley Road
Otley
LS21 3JP

Reprinted 1989
Reprinted 1992

I.S.B.N. 1 870071 20 4

Printed and bound by
Smith Settle
Ilkley Road
Otley

FOREWORD TO THE 1988 EDITION

To embark on the research for this book the authors bought a caravan, and the Green Plover, as it was christened, became familiar to many people in Wensleydale in the year 1935. Having approved of *Swaledale*, they were anxious to see a similar book on their own dale, so that we were generously helped and made many lasting friendships. We started our pilgrimage in the spring at the head of the dale, parked the caravan for the summer at Bainbridge, and in the autumn continued work in the lower dale.

As we read the book, compiled and written over fifty years ago, the recollections hint at Victorian and even Georgian times. Observations on many subjects — farming, lead-mining, the knitting industry, cheese-making, traditions, dialect — which have since been enlarged on, were then enriched by a greater closeness to the old life than we can encounter today.

Fifty years later much has changed. The Wensleydale line, once so important a part of life in the dale, closed in 1954; Yorebridge grammar school has become the Wensleydale school at Leyburn; Askrigg Old Hall was burnt down in 1935; Lunds church is closed; Bolton Castle has been refurbished, and the Upper Dales Folk Museum started at Hawes. Parts of Alexander Fothergill's diary have come to light, and new information on the first site of Askrigg church and of Blondin visiting

Hardraw qualify these two statements. Little farms in the remote dales have been amalgamated into larger holdings. Weekend cottages abound, and tourism is vigorously promoted. Wensleydale, Ella Pontefract emphasises, is a dale of villages, and it is still 'one of England's green valleys'.

For this new edition Marie Hartley has had the opportunity to make a few minor corrections.

NOTE

It has been our aim in this book to give a picture of Wensleydale as it is to-day, with a background of events in the past which have directly influenced the present.

We appreciate the help which has been generously given us, and wish to thank particularly Mr. Ernest E. Taylor for advice, Mr. J. J. G. Lodge for the loan of documents, Mr. R. M. Chapman for giving the result of his research into the early history and for reading over the manuscript, Mr. T. C. Calvert for information about Hawes, Mr. J. T. Leyland for help with the dialect, Mr. T. W. Grubb, Mr. T. Allen, Mr. H. Skidmore, Mr. J. A. Willis, Mr. E. Webster, Mr. F. Rodwell, Mrs. Ryder for recollections of old customs and stories, Mr. T. and Mr. C. Peacock for lead mining and other information, Mr. A. Rowntree for the use of early Quaker records, Miss J. G. Topham and Dr. G. Cockcroft for stories and introductions to Middleham and Coverdale. It is impossible to name all who have been willing to assist in preserving a record of the past and present life of the dale. We regret that it is only to the memory of Mr. R. A. Scott Macfie that our gratitude can go for details of the local history of Lunds and for the use of his library.

We have lived in many parts of Wensleydale in our caravan, 'The Green Plover,' and wish also to thank those on whose land it has stood, and all who by their kindliness and hospitality have made our work a pleasure.

E. P.

May 1936.   M. H.

CONTENTS

LIST OF ILLUSTRATIONS

WOOD-ENGRAVINGS

MAPS AND PLANS

LIST OF BOOKS CONSULTED

Wensleydale; or, Rural Contemplations, T. Maude (1816)
History of Richmondshire, Whitaker (1823)
The Wensleydale Advertiser (1844–7)
The Three Days of Wensleydale, W. G. M. J. Barker (1854)
A Month in Yorkshire, Walter White (1858)
History of Askrigg, C. Whaley (1890)
Romantic Richmondshire, H. Speight (1897)
Papers relating to the Lead Mines in Wensleydale, J. Backhouse
Seventeenth-century Life in a Country Parish, Eleanor Trotter (1919)
The Place-names of the North Riding, A. H. Smith
The Glaciation of Wensleydale and Swaledale, A. Raistrick
The Archaeology of Yorkshire, F. and H. Wragg Elgee
Victoria County History

Askrigg and Wether Fell

CHAPTER I

WENSLEYDALE

WENSLEYDALE in Yorkshire is one of England's green valleys. You find the greenness from the beginning, as soon as the River Ure, after its first rush down Lunds Fell, takes the decisive bend which is to lead it through Yorkshire, instead of the gentler way of the Eden into Westmorland. It is a narrow line of cultivation at first, and the moor creeps down as if it would snatch it back to itself, but there are, nevertheless, meadows where grass is grown for hay, and pastures where cattle feed. Swiftly, as the valley dips and widens, the grass-land increases, running in more level fields and climbing further up the fells, growing ever more luxuriant, to become at length some of the finest grazing land in the country. Near the foot of the dale a few ploughed

1

fields appear, but these grow chiefly turnips and potatoes, so that they too are green for much of the year.

It is a grassy dale, and only for a few weeks in summer when the grass ripens does it change its face. Then the fields have their time of glory, to the making of which the whole year has gone. They are pink where the grass is still uncut, brown where hay is drying, yellow where it has just been led, and darkening where the grass begins to grow again.

The trees intensify the greenness, exaggerating the brightness by their dark outlines in the winter, showing it sombre and discreet when they burst into their spring freshness, and joining with it in the summer as if to flaunt the many shades and changes which this colour can achieve. They too grow in the higher reaches, scattered, except where they climb the ravines or have been planted in clumps to break the wind, and always with a definite line above which they do not go. They follow the river on its downward journey, dotting themselves ever thicker in the meadows, until in the lower dale they attain a density which gives the valley the appearance of a park.

Through this green land the River Ure flows unobtrusively, cutting for the most part a silent, easy course, but in the one stretch where rocks bar its way, breaking into some of the finest waterfalls in England. But it is a dale river, fed by becks which drain from the fells, and its normal, almost noiseless flow can change suddenly after storms to a torrent, flooding fields and roads and houses near its banks.

The fells which shut in Wensleydale, and without

which it would not be a dale, emphasize its green fertility. They do not overshadow the valley, it is in most places too wide; nor, except for one ridge on the north, do they run up it in an unbroken line like a barrier, there are too many smaller dales cutting through them to allow for that. They do not rely for beauty on the turns and twists of the valley, for this is not a winding dale. It is the shape of them which is their attraction. They rise into isolated peaks, many of which end a ridge bounding a smaller dale. As a proverb says: 'There is a hill against a dale all Wensleydale over.' Their cliff-like faces often end in a series of terraces, formed by the wearing away of the softer layers of rock. Each has its own characteristics, and each dominates a stretch of the dale. You find yourself measuring your way up or down by them, Witton Fell, Penhill, Addle-borough, Wether Fell, Cotter End. As one is left behind another appears, itself changing as the road passes it. But when they are named, it is a particular shape which comes into mind, as the dome-like summit of Penhill, or the crouching face of Cotter End. In their individuality and difference they are almost human, and you come to love them as you would love a person. They present an ever-changing background to the green valley, from the almost monotonous green of those summer weeks when the line between it and them is nearly indistinguishable, to their autumn abandonment of rusts, ambers, and purples, and their various winter moods when under their covering of bleached grass and rushes they seem to shrink into themselves, or white with snow sparkling in the sunshine, they appear to expand and take to themselves the impenetrable look of mountains. But they are friendly hills, even the wildest of them.

When you think of the fells of Wensleydale you think at the same time of the villages which lie under them: West Witton sheltering beneath Penhill, Bainbridge looking up to Addleborough, Askrigg under the scarry slope of Ellerkin. They are bound up with each other. The stone for the cottages and barns was quarried from their sides, and on them feed the sheep and cattle, the breeding and rearing of which is still the main industry of the people. They belong to them as much as to the green valley: East Witton lining its hilly green, Middleham with its grim castle ruin, Redmire with its look of age, beautiful West Burton, quaint Appersett; you could name them all and still call them beautiful. They are villages and little towns, each with a distinct life of its own, but each consciously a part of the whole dale, and reflecting its spirit. You see these villages in the distance as little clumps up both sides of the valley, sometimes brown and clear showing dark against the green, sometimes in a soft haze as the smoke of their own chimneys settles over them, sometimes as groups of lights in the darkness. Often two of them come near together like sisters, as Hawes and Gayle, Bainbridge and Askrigg, Redmire and Castle Bolton. It is significant that Wensleydale was not called after its river, as are most of the Yorkshire dales, but after what was once an important market town, and is now a tiny village. You can forget that one particular place was picked out, and think of it as the dale of villages.

And there are the smaller dales, Coverdale, Bishopdale, Raydale, Cotterdale, and innumerable still smaller ones. They are like the branches of a big family of which Wensleydale is the head. Some are miniatures of her graciousness and repose; some have a fierce, untamed beauty, which far exceeds her wildest moods; some rest quiet and secure in their own loveliness; some are shut away like secret, forgotten valleys. They have an unexpected quality. Wandering about them you realize something of what Wensleydale itself was like in quieter, less restless days than these. Customs and sayings survive in them which are only memories here. Each has its separate life, but each is also centred in the town or village which, standing at or near its foot, links it up with the bigger dale.

This is Wensleydale as you find it to-day. There seems a permanency about it, as if it had always been this green fertile valley under sheltering fells, with people settling there and villages growing up, because it was a good place to live in. But like most parts of England, it has been made as it is by man. One of its fascinations lies in the fact that traces of the succeeding groups of people who inhabited it are there for the seeking, not built on or destroyed. Some are obvious, some so hidden away that the search for them becomes an adventure. You find them in the valleys and near the rivers, and the hills are scarred with them. Once you begin there is no end, for this, the largest of the Yorkshire dales, has had a more eventful past than the others.

There are remains of dwellings, stone circles, and

implements of the people of the Bronze Age who lived here three thousand years ago; there is evidence of a Roman fort at Bainbridge, and the roads which led to it; there are foundations of Saxon villages, and signs of their methods of cultivation. The Norsemen survive in the names of the villages, fields, and becks. With the Normans came the abbeys, churches, and castles. The settling of the monks after the Conquest had most to do with the making of the dale as we know it. They farmed the land, built mills, and developed industries which continued long after their abbeys were dissolved.

For centuries the land, except round the villages and vaccaries, was waste, used by the earls for hunting boars and deer. It was known as the Forest of Wensleydale, but the meaning of the word 'forest' has changed, and this was chiefly open moorland with wooded stretches fenced off for preserving game, called 'parks.' The trees, except in the parks, were low bushes. Some of these can still be seen in the ravines and along the sides of the scars.

Gradually the clearings were extended, but it was in the seventeenth century that the reclaiming of the land went on with the greatest speed. It was then that many of the farmhouses and manors were rebuilt. Often they have the date and the initials of the builder over their doors, some crudely carved, others finely decorated and with mouldings up the sides. These generally come in groups, in a particular village or district, and show that here were skilful and inventive masons. Seeing one, you imagine that house when it was built and lived in nearly three hundred years ago, and guess at the name of the people. If the parish registers go back far enough, you can often find them there, and see when they were married, when their children were born, and when they died.

Farming was always the main occupation. In the early days herds of pigs were grazed in the forest in such numbers that the settlements near them were called after them, as Swineley and Swineside. But it developed into the sheep and dairy farming for which it is famous to-day. The dale has given its name to a particular kind of cheese which is never the same when not made from Wensleydale milk, from cows fed on limestone land, and to a breed of sheep, long-wooled Wensleydales which are known in all parts of the world.

As the farms grew the dale became richer, and new industries were started, and old ones were extended, so that it was largely self-supporting. It grew its own corn; you can see the waves of the plough furrows in the flat meadows: 'rigg and furr,' the people call them. Old field names, the 'Corn Closes' and 'Pluin's,' are relics of this time. It ground all the corn for its own use and a great deal for Swaledale, Wharfedale, and Ribblesdale. Nearly every village had its corn-mill. The ruins of some can still be seen, but of many only the memory remains. A few were turned into worsted or cotton mills; those which are left are now chiefly saw-mills or dairies.

Craftsmen sprang up, woolcombers, coopers, clockmakers; and there were knitters. Before the days of machinery men, women, and children knitted, first with wool which they spun themselves, and later with wool spun in the mills. And in many parts there was lead mining. This industry started before the Romans came; some of the Roman roads were made for the carrying of lead. The story of its progress is shown on the scoured slopes of the fells, from the very early tippings now grown with grass and heather to the latest ones still bare and ugly, and the ruined smelt mills which were not closed until the end of the nineteenth century. Coal too was found and worked in the hills.

With the growth of the dale the markets and fairs developed. Wensleydale, lying as it does between Swaledale and Upper Wharfedale, and with an easy approach at its upper end, made itself a centre for the other two dales, drawing buyers and sellers from their more isolated districts.

All this business and outside communication meant more roads. There had from the first settlements been tracks in Wensleydale. The early Britons made them; some of the Roman roads were theirs improved. The Roman road over Wether Fell is one of the most stirring sights in the dale. You see it from the other side of the valley, cutting its unswerving way over the fell, its grassy surface showing clear and distinct against the darker growth. These old roads run in all directions over the hills; they went seldom in the valley, which would be thick with undergrowth and subject to floods. They lead into other dales, to the coal and lead mines, and down to the villages; old jagging roads along which cattle drovers came, packmen brought their goods, and coal and corn and lead were carried. As people began to understand drainage, roads were made lower down the hillsides, and the old ways became the grassy tracks which are one of the joys of Wensleydale. A few are overgrown, and have almost disappeared into the moor, but these can be picked up and followed here and there like some forgotten puzzle. The new roads became turnpike roads up which the coaches ran, and they in their turn have become the modern highways.

In 1844 a fortnightly newspaper called the *Wensleydale Advertiser* was started in Hawes, and ran until 1849, when it was sold, not, we are told, because of lack of support. It gives a picture of the dale in the middle of the nineteenth century, showing it curiously like and yet unlike the dale of to-day. The people were using old roads, but planning new ones and rebuilding bridges; improving the coach services, but anticipating the railway, not so very far away at Northallerton: keeping up the old fairs, but regretting that much of the zest in them had gone; enjoying a new entertainment in the tea galas originated by young and enthusiastic temperance societies, and held at beauty spots like Aysgarth Falls and Leyburn Shawl. The lead mines were busy, rising to their zenith; the farms were still being improved by draining and liming. But there was great poverty amongst the working people. The knitters worked incessantly, and got only fourpence a pair for knitting large, high stockings; other workers knitted in their spare time to eke out a living. But the poor people helped each other; if a man's cow died the whole village would club together to help him buy another; if there was illness it became the personal responsibility of each inhabitant. Life was a struggle, but it developed

ingenuity. One man who had a donkey made a cart and
painted it red and yellow. An envious neighbour said:
'Aye, Tom's meeade 'issel' a cart, an' 'e'd 'ave meeade
a donkey too if 'e could.'

There was joy when the railway was first projected,
although the people were agitated about the strange men
who were to invade the dale. They pressed for better
prisons and more constables; the constables at that time
were local men quite untrained. Little by little the
iron lines crept up it, reaching Leyburn in 1856, Askrigg
in 1877, and Hawes in 1878; old people can remember
the celebrations as each new piece was opened. In 1871
the Midland Railway took their line from Settle to
Carlisle through its upper part at Lunds, and later the
line up the valley was extended to meet it at Hawes
Junction. Years of work and the loss of many lives
went to the making of it.

As the local train crawls almost unnoticed up the
valley it seems natural that the line should be where it is.
But this was only one of many schemes, for railway
speculators, Hudson amongst them, saw the possibilities
of Wensleydale, and saw some of them glorified. For
months the dale was measured and surveyed; if all the
plans had materialized, it would have resembled the
nursery floor of a child with a taste for lines and engines.
Four railways were planned up the valley, two on each
side of the river; one to cut miles through the hill into
Swaledale; one to tunnel to Buckden in Wharfedale;
one to cross above Aysgarth Falls; and one to pass
Semerwater into Wharfedale.

In comparison the railway which did arrive seems

inoffensive, but its effects were great. It brought navvies in hundreds while it was being made, it brought regular workers to reside in the dale, it gave work to dales-people. And it brought the Victorian day tripper. We envy the Victorian tripper; it must all have been so fresh and exciting. The travellers in the coaches had been for the most part passers-by on their way to Kirkby Stephen, Kendal, Lancaster, and the Lake District, who as a rule stayed in the towns only while the horses were being changed, but these new travellers came in crowds, to marvel at the falls of Hardraw and Aysgarth, and the view from Leyburn Shawl. The dale was known when Swaledale and Upper Wharfedale were too remote for any but enthusiastic walkers. It became a holiday resort.

And so it has gone on; after the trains came cycles, cars, buses. How spoilt it all might have been, and how little it really is. Modern ideas there are, but they are a top veneer. Underneath is the dale character and tra-dition, not needing the outside world to make its life complete. It has the essentials.

One evening in late autumn as we sat outside our caravan under the slope of Shunnor Fell, a burst of jazz music came suddenly from nowhere. It had an incon-gruous sound in the quiet country. Then on the road above Appersett we saw a lighted bus, and realized that its wireless was switched on. The noise grew louder as it drew level, then faded as the bus ran down to Hawes. As it vanished a shepherd called to his dog on the moor, and the alien visions it had brought were forgotten in an instant as the tranquillity and sufficiency of the valley folded round us again.

If the dalespeople who lived before the days of the railway could come back they would see differences. They would find the lead and coal mines and the stone quarries closed, and their place taken by limestone quarries. They would find the old industries, the knitting and the clockmaking gone. They would be astonished to find a newer means of transport than the railway, and smooth tarred roads to carry it. They would find the markets bigger, but the village feasts a mere echo of the feasts they knew. There would be fewer people in the dale, and we think that they would miss most of all the farmhouses, the homes of some of them, now derelict or made into barns. They would find the farming changed, but would still see the cows, in ever-increasing numbers, owing to the new milk conditions. Cows are everywhere, adding their colour and placidity to each scene. The sight and sound and smell of them fill the dale in summer.

They would see the villages little altered. And surely they would still feel at home in that completeness of the dale and its people in themselves. You must realize this self-sufficiency to understand Wensleydale and its people to-day. To many of them the limits of their dale are still the limits of their world. In that world they are among friends. When they were more isolated there was so much intermarrying that now, particularly in the upper dale, nearly all are related. In times of trouble or joy they are like one big family. They are loyal to their dale, their own village in it, and to each other. They have an independence which is refreshing. The farmers, however small their farms, are their own masters, their success or failure depends on themselves and their decisions. They are never lacking in a quick reply. A man pointing out a short cut to us was interrupted by another who said there was a bull in the field. 'Gad,' said the first, 'then I wadn't go for a cheese.' Thomas Gent in the eighteenth century described them as

> An hardy people, far above Ure's Rills,
> Content with lowly food on lofty Hills.

You do not find the lowly food now, but the contentment and the lofty hills are theirs still.

So through the centuries the dale has attained graciousness. Its development has been so slow that it has come with naturalness. It has a restful quality, lulling you into content with itself. Its beauty spots are worth the fame they have achieved, but for those who dislike the well known there are others tucked away in corners about which little has been said. The main roads offer bold, grand sweeps, the unfolding valley, and the beckoning hills, but close by are unsophisticated corners, so many that some you alone will discover. These will stay in your memory because of the mood in which you found them or the jovial word with which some dalesman sent you on your way to them. You can visit them again and again and never see them quite the same, for this is a valley of changing effects, of light and shadow made by sun and wind and rain on the hills.

The Children's Roundabout

CHAPTER II

HAWES

HAWES is the Mecca of the upper dale. From all directions roads meet in or near it—the passes of Greensett and the Buttertubs, the roads from Sedbergh and Kirkby Stephen, and the roads up the dale. Its name, coming from the word *hals*, means a neck or pass between mountains. It was originally 'The Hawes,' and in dialect is still called 'T' Haas.' The more dignified name suits its air of importance and purpose. It seems natural for traffic to stop in this centre.

Hawes is not old, there was little of it when places which are now quiet villages had busy markets. It has no particular beauty, only the charm of a place admirably suited for its purpose. It manages perfectly its dual role of market town for the upper dale, and a holiday

place for tourists. For these last its hotels are enlarged,
but that is the only concession, it is too busy with its
own life to do more. You must take it as you find it,
and for that reason you never tire of Hawes.

If you enter from the east end, narrow, winding
streets lead you to the broad market-place. If you come
down from the west, houses and chimneys far below tell
of a community to welcome you. This welcome from
the hills is one of its great attractions; cosy rooms after
windswept moors, roofs and shelter which they denied;
twinkling lights cheerful in the growing dusk; rest from
the hot summer sun. The town is cradled in hills.
They are all around, waiting to be discovered, and
seeming to creep up in protection when evening comes.
It is one with the hills, its life depends on them, and
the men who live amongst them.   Once, during fair
week in October, we were in a shop in Hawes when a
gipsy woman came in to buy a post card. 'You know,'
she said, as she turned the cards, 'we like this place,
we like scenery better than sea.'

You never lose your wonder at finding a town so high
up the dale. Only a mile beyond it the last village is
left, and the roads climb to the moors. A breath of
their adventure and freedom pervades its streets. It creeps
into the shops, those which are grocers, confectioners, and
drapers combined, and those filled with rope and sheep
dip. It is felt in the post office, which is business-like
and efficient on one side, and on the other a place in
which to linger.   In between the shops houses are wedged;
one with an outside staircase shows a little of what Hawes
was like at the beginning of the nineteenth century.

The church stands in its churchyard high above the main road; its tower with a turret on one corner is a familiar sight from all sides, making the town easy to distinguish from a distance. It was built in 1850 to replace a smaller church which stood lower down the churchyard, and of which there is an engraving in the vestry. The first mention of a church in Hawes is a record that in 1483 Richard III appointed 'Sir James Whalley, priest, to sing at the Chapelle of the Haws in Wensladale for oon yere and for his salary hath given him seven marks.'

The Quaker meeting-house, established in 1695, and its burial ground are near the station. The Quakers were strong in Wensleydale, and Hawes was one of their centres. A lady remembers as a child being taken to Meeting with her sister by their grandmother, in the days when dresses were worn closely buttoned up the back. The hour went by without any one speaking, and all that broke the silence were the sighs of the two little girls, and the noise of their buttons creaking on the back of the seat as they fidgeted.

A house standing back from the road behind a garden was a Quaker rest-house, where people coming from a distance could rest and eat between Meetings. Over the door is the inscription:

Ano Dom 1668
God being with us
Who canbe against.

A
T F.

The Duerley beck coming down from Gayle flows

through this east end of the town, crossed by a narrow bridge. The building above it, once a woollen mill, is now partly used as a cheese dairy, and the old bleaching yard has been made into a piggery attached to it. In the other half the town's electricity is made, the power coming from the beck. There are similar dairies down the dale, bringing the derelict mills into use again, and keeping in the dale work which belongs to it.

Milk is to-day the most important product of the farms. Ever since the railway came some milk has gone out of the dale in liquid form. A train known as the 'Milk Train' used to take it direct to London every night; later the Express Dairy contracted for a certain amount, and this was sent by train to Appleby in Westmorland, to be pasteurized before going to London. Also local dairies were opened—the one at Hawes was established in 1898, but farmers in the outlying districts still made their own cheese and butter. When the Milk Marketing Board came into operation in 1933 most of the farmers found it would pay them better to sell their milk; and now lorries collect it from all parts of the dale. It is roughly estimated that, besides the milk taken by the local dairies, six thousand gallons go to London every day from that part of Wensleydale between Lunds and Leyburn.

Except on a few isolated farms the day seems to have gone when the farmers' wives made cheese and butter, and with it has gone some of the romance of the farmhouses when rows of cheeses stood in the cheese rooms, and butter and cream on the dairy shelves. But cheese-making, which had to be done every morning from May

c

to September, was heavy work. As soon as the milk came in it was put into a large 'cheese kettle,' heated to a certain temperature, and rennet added to separate the curds and whey. In earlier days 'keslops,' the stomach of a calf pickled and stretched on two sticks to dry, was used instead of rennet. The curds were then kneaded, pressed into moulds, and put into cheese presses where they stayed for the night before being placed on the cheese-room shelves to dry. Here they had to be turned daily, and the dry ones dusted, a long business as the summer advanced.

The process is the same in the dairies, but zinc-lined vats running on wheels have taken the place of the 'cheese kettles,' and the work is a wholetime job. The big dairies can manage their markets better. Cheeses to-day are often sold new, but the farmer had to wait until late autumn when they had dried and lost weight to sell his, and he had as a rule to accept the shopkeeper's or dealer's price when he came round to bargain for them.

Whilst cheese was still being made in the farmhouses the old stone presses had given way to iron ones. You see the blocks of stone, often with the iron hook left, leant against outbuildings or built into walls, just as you see the old millstones, whose day also has gone, made into flags and steps.

These parts of Hawes lie close to the main road, but there are yards and cobbled alleys opening from it which the passer-by misses, and curving out from the north side is the Holme, a broad, clean street with a quiet, rather decorous air, and where big and little houses mingle with the delightful jumble of a country town.

It was in the Holme that the fortnightly newspaper, the *Wensleydale Advertiser*, started by Mr. Fletcher Clark in 1844, was printed and published. It was the first stamped, and therefore the first legal, newspaper in the North Riding. Its early numbers were models of what a local newspaper should be. It declared that its aim was to tell, not so much the happenings of the world outside, as the everyday life of the dale.

The *Darlington and Stockton Times* has taken the place of the *Wensleydale Advertiser* in the dale. It is 'the farmer's Bible.' 'It's i' t' Darlin'ton,' he says, and thereby settles any dispute. One Saturday we called to see an old man, and found him sitting in his doorway reading a newspaper. He is generally ready to talk, but that day he seemed distracted. 'I were just readin' t' Darlin'ton,' he said, 'an' it taks me meeast o' Setturday to git through it.'

The use of broad dialect has declined in the dale. A stranger will not hear it spoken generally, though many people use it naturally to each other, and it is still strong in the smaller dales. Hawes has in Mr. John Thwaite a local dialect poet to keep the old words alive. A few examples are: 'kye' (cows), 'lile' (little), 'terrible'—pronounced 'terble'—(very), 'snizy' (bitterly cold), 'dowly' (dull), 'mague' (mist), 'shive' (slice), 'ket' (rubbish).

Hawes to-day is first and foremost a market town; the market is the reason for its size and importance, almost the meaning of its existence. It did not get its market charter until 1700, when William III granted to 'Matthew Wetherald, Gentleman, the right to hold a weekly market in the town of Hawes, and two fairs

annually.' Slowly from that time the smaller markets
of the dale became merged in this or Leyburn market.
Their character has changed; the sheep and cattle are no
longer sold by private bargaining in the streets, but by
auction in the Auction Mart. Much that was picturesque
has gone with the old markets: the farmers, silent and
wary, bargaining with each other largely by signs; the
pens in the market - place; the streets crowded with
moving sheep and cattle, massed so thickly together that
men with sticks were employed to keep them out of the
shops. But the gatherings in the Auction Mart are still
essentially of the dale. Everybody knows everybody,
and all about the stock which is to be sold.

The women are now more cut off from the men.
They are busy at the stalls, and seldom penetrate into
the fuggy sheds of the Auction Mart at the other end
of the town. Apart from their own job of feeding the
calves, making butter, and helping with the hay, most
of them leave the business of the farms to the men.

The most important fairs are in the autumn. There
is a Bull Fair when powerful beasts are led through the
streets, and the air resounds with their bellowing.
Special sheep fairs follow of stock which the farmer
does not wish to keep through the winter. Much of it
comes from Swaledale; all the day before and in the early
morning of the fair day little flocks of sheep are driven
over the Buttertubs Pass, a sight which with its essential
lack of hurry is a tonic in these days. Moor ponies
were once sold at the fair to dealers who had them shod,
and then took them to sell again at Brough Hill Fair in
Westmorland a few days later.

Pictures of the fair linger in the mind: a dog barking excitedly round a flock of ewes as they round the corner by the station; a stall near by with ropes and leather goods hung round it; two pleasant-looking daleswomen turning an appraising eye on the fruit and vegetable stall; an intent group inside the ring in the mart, absent-mindedly pushing back with their sticks a cow which endeavours to find a way out. 'Aye,' an old farmer informed us, 'it's a wonnerful place is t' Haas. Ther's a deal o' money turned ower thar in a year.'

A feast was always held at the time of Hawes Fair. People came from all parts, and thieves and pickpockets came too. There is an item in the account book of the Constabulary of Bainbridge for 1798: 'To journey and Expences with 2 Highwaymen taken at the Hawes fare as Acct. £2 -19 -10.' The feast is now only a round-about, a few stalls and fortune-tellers' tents in a field, and a children's roundabout.

You find this children's roundabout at most of the autumn fairs. We saw it making its way to Hawes pulled by a horse. Once there, its owner disdained the fair ground, and put it up in the main street. It is worked by hand, and the rides vary—short and quick if more are waiting for a turn, slower and longer if the owner is having an interesting conversation with any one. He likes to talk about his life on the roads, how he starts out in the spring, and never goes back until the autumn fairs are over, when he settles for the winter in a Durham town. He does his own cooking, and has strong ideas about food, never using 'tinned stuff.' There are interruptions in his conversation for unloading and loading the roundabout and waiting for final instructions to children who are having their first taste of a fair.

Formerly dances were held on the fair and feasts nights. There were four inns at Hawes with rooms big enough for dancing, and which were known as 'long rooms.' Dancing began at six o'clock at night, and went on until six o'clock in the morning. The music was supplied by a concertina, mouth-organ, or fiddle, the fiddle being the most popular. Each man paid a penny a dance to the musician. If the room was not very full a longer dance would be given for the penny. News of this would spread, and the room would soon be crowded, when short measure was given again, and the dancers were induced by similar tales to go back to the other inns. As the evening wore on men became reckless; one out of a wage of half a crown a day spent four shillings on dances, so that he must have managed to step through forty-eight. Hawes still dances, but in less hilarious mood.

Some farmers who have taken to dealing in cattle have made fortunes. A successful cattle dealer living a few miles from Hawes always carried a large quantity of money about with him, generally in his boots. One market-day a farmer refused to take a cheque in payment for some sheep. The buyer had not the amount in ready money with him, but the Hawes dealer offered to take the cheque, and produced the money from inside his boots, by no means using all he was carrying. These men with a knack of making money have often had no ambition to change their way of living. The same man, as soon as he arrived home from the market, wrote his accounts on the whitewashed wall of his kitchen. Having worked them out to his own satisfaction he fetched a bucket of whitewash, which was always kept in a corner, and with a sweep of the brush covered up the reckonings. That was his only method of book-keeping, though he had been known to sell a hundred cattle in a day. When he died he was found to be worth twenty thousand pounds, and the value of his furniture was given as five pounds. The discrepancy of the two amounts roused the suspicion of the authorities, and inspectors were sent to the house. They found the farm kitchen, which was also the living room, as it had been in the man's poorest days, with the whitewashed walls which he had found so useful.

The river lies to the north of the town where Brunt Acres Road, on the way to Hardraw, crosses it over Haylands Bridge. A bridge here in 1607 was said to be 'in great ruin and decaie.' Before 1820, when the present bridge was made for a carriage way, wheeled vehicles had to cross a ford which still remains a right of way; near it the inhabitants had the privilege of getting water and sand. The walls of the bridge are pierced to break the force of the water in times of flood, for the Ure, calm and safe normally, floods rapidly after storms, turning the valley here into a vast lake, and making both roads to Hardraw impassable.

There have been many controversies about the name of the river. The earliest recorded name was 'Earp,' which had become 'Jor' in 1142, thus giving its name to Jervaulx (Jorvale) Abbey. It was 'Yeure' in 1530, but the Tudor historians, Leland and Camden, called it 'Ure,' as do present-day maps. The old name survives in Yorebridge, near Bainbridge; in names of farmhouses like Yorescott; and in Yorburgh, one of the buttresses of Wether Fell. But this is Wensleydale in the twentieth century and, however much you prefer 'Yore,' it is more convenient to spell it 'Ure.'

The area round Haylands Bridge seems to be the playground of the upper dale. There are generally fishermen standing in the river, for there is excellent trout and grayling fishing. On one side is the cricket field, its closely cut pitch a vivid green against the marshy grass, and on the other is a nine-hole golf course, with bunkers and hazards ready made.

A flagged path goes back across the fields to Hawes. Flagged paths are a feature of this part of Wensleydale. Firmly embedded in the earth, and worn by generations, they seem to have been there for ever, like the towns and villages, and like them they are examples of the using of local material for the everyday needs of life, and so creating harmony. They were put for a definite purpose, for where there is a flagged way the grass does not get worn on either side as it does round trodden paths. They lead to the villages which lie round Hawes like satellites, Hardraw, Burtersett, and Gayle, villages which wait to be discovered and explored.

Lunds Church

CHAPTER III

LUNDS AND THE SOURCE OF THE URE

THE Ure rises in country very different from that which it has reached at Hawes—wilder, grimmer country with much that is primeval about it. The road from Hawes climbs always to the fells, and after six miles the valley turns at the Moorcock Inn into the district of Lunds, which is in the very heart of them. It is a valley cut off from and unlike anything else in Wensleydale.

The present road from the inn to Shaw Paddock, on the way to Kirkby Stephen, was not made until 1825. The older one is on the hill across the valley, where it can be traced along the ridge. The real Lunds lies there, in the farmhouses, some of which are seen from the road, dotted along the hillside. These you will discover later. You may even come to think that away from them the road has the loneliness and lack of life of many

25

modern roads which avoid the villages and hamlets. But on your first journey you will not mind if the road is old or new, built on or deserted; it will carry you along with its own excitement. If you love the fells, you will love it, for it runs chiefly on their lower slopes. They shut the valley in on all sides, Grisedale and Swarth Fells on the west, Abbotside Common rising to High Seat on the east, and in front the bulk of Wild Boar Fell.

Wild Boar Fell, rearing itself as a barrier between Yorkshire and Westmorland, is a background to the valley. It is not an insuperable barrier; it seems to invite you on to see what lies round the corner, to the solemn ridge of Mallerstang Edge, with its crags and scars, and the radiant valley of the Eden, with its border castles. Its outline of flat top and scar-like edges so impresses itself on the mind that, even if it is faint in a haze of heat or shrouded by mist and rain, you seem to see it clearly.

As you travel this road you find that a little of the life of the valley drifts up to it. The school is here now, and the way turning down to Lunds church. In June peat is cut close beside it. The dark figures of the men cutting and paring it and rearing the blocks one against another to dry move slowly and silently on the unpeopled fell, and seem symbolical of this settlement whose roots are far in the past. Square hollows show where they have taken peat in other years, and on the marshy land around them cotton flowers wave their heads.

Alongside the road there is the railway, part of the line from Settle to Carlisle. You see it first just beyond the Moorcock Inn on the Sedbergh road, crossing the

road and the head of the Garsdale valley on a lofty
viaduct. The line as it curves into Lunds is on such a
stupendous scale that it seems in sympathy with the
surrounding vastness, and compensates a little for its
intrusion. Trains rushing through the valley on their
way to and from London disturb its peace only for a
moment. Travellers looking out from dining coaches
behold this expanse in which the figures of men, if they
see them at all, must look like pigmies. The line has
been the scene of two disastrous accidents: on Christmas
Eve, 1910, and in the summer of 1913, all the more
terrible because of the remoteness and isolation of the
valley.

During the making of the line from 1871 to 1876 an
alien life came temporarily into the dale. The hundreds
employed on it and in quarrying stone for bridges and
viaducts had to be housed, and wooden villages grew up
at intervals. The people who came to live in them were
a rough, mixed lot to be planted here, where families
had lived for generations. Inns opened for their benefit
were the scenes of brawls and fights, when the floors
were said to run with blood. But their wooden houses
have gone, and almost all remembrance of them. There
remain only some unmarked mounds in the churchyard,
and unfamiliar names in the parish registers, whose entries
were more frequent during those years.

And then the road comes to Shaw Paddock, which,
although an isolated house, seems a centre of this
district. It is below the old road, but a track comes down
from it, and at this point the farms have spread to the
west side of the valley. There must have been an early

dwelling here, for 'shaw' means wood, and 'paddock' is a modern corrupt form of the Anglo-Saxon word 'parrock,' an enclosure. It is still called Shaw Parrock by the dalespeople. Further up the road is the last farm-house in Yorkshire, White Birks, where the only signs of white birches to-day are the trunks of these trees buried in the peat.

Shaw Paddock is one of those peaceful farmhouses of which we think with longing when we are in other places. We remember its bright fireside, and the talks round it; its V-shaped dairy, with rows of butter and bowls of milk on the shelves; its window at the back looking to the hill where the River Ure rises. It stands at an angle from the road, and the space in front seems made for lingering. Tradesmen journeying from Hawes to Kirkby Stephen rest their horses here for a time; people from the farms across the valley leave their cycles in its spacious barns; the egg man comes with his van and exchanges groceries for baskets of eggs, and the butter man does the same with the butter, and neither is in any hurry to leave.

Perhaps it is some of the old hospitality of an inn which clings round it, for up to the end of the last century the house was an inn. It was known generally as Shaw Paddock Inn, but for a period round 1827 it was called 'The Bull.' Drovers put up here on their way to the fairs. Wild characters have sat in its inn parlour, and if the walls could speak they would tell tales of missing men and shots in the night never accounted for.

We had our caravan across the road in a little field, which we call the hospital, because the few weakly lambs are brought into it to be nursed. Twice a day the farmer comes in, catches each lamb in turn with a long shepherd's crook, and forces it to feed either from its mother or from a bottle. The shepherd's crook is home-made from a long tree branch, the fork of the branch, beautifully smoothed, forming the crook.

The hills which shut in the valley on the east are the watersheds of three rivers, the Ure, the Eden, and the Swale. The Ure and the Eden on the west side flow towards each other until, when only a narrow space divides them, the Eden turns north into Westmorland and the Ure south into Yorkshire. The Ure takes its name from the beginning, but the Eden is known at first as Hell Gill Beck. For a time it forms the county boundary of Yorkshire, which crosses the road by Aisgill Cottages. Dick Turpin is said to have jumped his horse over it, escaping from justice out of Westmorland. A bridge crosses the beck, and beyond it stands the farmhouse of Hell Gill, with its ring of pastures and meadows bordered on all sides by the moor. The stream cuts its way through a deep gorge, and emerges on a bed of flat rock to plunge as a waterfall into a pool below. This first headstrong piece of the Eden was the original source of the Ure, but glacial drift at the end of the Ice Age silted up the river-bed, and it was diverted by means of the fall into the Eden. The present beginnings of the Ure, if less adventurous, are more typical of the river which it is to become.

From Ure Head, or Sails (2,186 ft.), the ridge of the hill rises to High Seat. There is a savage solitude here, and a freedom which exhilarates. Man, except to plant his stone pikes on the ridges, has had no hand in its making. The memory of it cheers and revitalizes in less uplifting places. But Ure Head gives one of those surprises which are characteristic of Wensleydale. On all sides are swelling hills, and to the east the ravines which are the beginnings of Cotterdale, but far away to the south-east there appear a stretch of meadow, a cluster of houses, and a church tower. You wonder what other dale you have suddenly glimpsed; then realize that, through the dip of the fells into Cotterdale, you are looking at the town of Hawes. So from the hill on which her river starts, Wensleydale shows her first town where the river is already broad and strong. Not for long does she let you forget her green valley and her villages.

The river rises as a trickle in the grass; now it cuts a feeble way through a stretch of peat; now struggles through rushes; now down a deep ravine. For a little way it runs underground, leaving its old bed dry with fallen rocks, and trees growing in the cracks, an eerie spot with its life, which was the river, gone. But it emerges, and comes, always winding, past its first little bridge to Ure Crook, named after that critical turn down the valley. Here, within sight of its first trickle, farmhouses appear, and the life which follows its course begins.

The track from Hell Gill to Shaw Paddock is a wide, grassy way, soft and springy to the feet, and you walk it with a swinging stride. If no one were to tread along it again it seems as if this would always be a green track, cropped like a lawn by sheep. You meet a herd of shaggy brown cattle with long horns and gentle faces—if you stand for a minute they walk curiously towards you; horses wintering on the fells gallop across, their long tails waving. Then you come to the first bridge over the Ure, a rough stone arch, with only a wooden rail for protection. Its name is Green Bridge.

In spring the track is a sanctuary for birds. The hill-side seems suddenly alive as a flock of golden plovers rises with a monotonous whistle, and settles again, hardly distinguishable from the moor. A pair of yellow wag-tails skim along and perch on a tuft of grass, as if they know how well their yellowy green plumage is displayed against that sombre background. Curlews give their liquid, burbling call, a call of pure happiness, the music of the fells. Seeing you, they swoop above, their long curved beaks opening and shutting as they utter a harsh, agitated cry, angry at your intrusion. On the moor the curlews are in pairs, their calls of joy or warning are to each other; but at evening they come down to the lower land to feed in flocks of as many as eighteen. Green plovers—'tewits,' the dalespeople call them, and explain them as 'them wi' toppin's'—cry excitedly above, revelling in the joy of motion. Snipe rise exultantly into the air, and swoop downwards with their peculiar drumming sound. The birds come suddenly to the moor. One day it is empty and silent, and the next they fill it with their life.

From the door of our caravan we have watched a heron flying slowly up the valley, its great wings spread out and seeming to glitter as they caught the rays of the sun. It looked magnificent, a creature of power. Later it would fish in the river, catching numbers of trout, and making itself disliked by the farmers who are fishermen, and who will shoot the 'hearinsew' if they can. It is a sign of bad weather when a heron comes as far up the valley as Lunds.

Perhaps as you arrive at the road you meet a shepherd driving his flock of sheep back to the fells after lambing time, their approach heralded by that sound which is only heard when sheep and lambs together are made to do unfamiliar things, a mingling of the low hoarse call of sheep and the treble bleating of lambs, a concentration of all their cries.

Before the lambs go up to the fell they are branded, so that they can mix with others on the common land. At Shaw Paddock this is done at the end of the lane, which can be partitioned off by two gates. They are marked with their owner's initial or sign in tar mixed with red paint. The sheep, which are not marked until after the shearing in July, remain outside to peer anxiously through the gate, and welcome back their offspring with murmurs of satisfaction.

It is generally in May, when the meadows are needed to grow for hay, that the lambs, then only three or four weeks old, are sent with their mothers to face the harder life of the fells. You see them everywhere, showing white and curly against the darker wool of the sheep. When, as so often in the spring, the wind is in the east, they shelter in the ravines and limestone hollows. Near the summit of Swarth Fell there is a flat tableland, where the wind seems to lull suddenly, and in wild weather the sheep remember this, and make for it with their lambs. These mountain sheep are hardy, and able to stand the weather. They soon become independent, though the hard life makes them serious; it is seldom that lambs play on the fells.

Every year in October a show for cattle and sheep is held in a field opposite the Moorcock Inn, for the farmers of this scattered district. This is the only show of its kind now held in Wensleydale. It generally rains, but nobody minds that. It is a leisurely affair; the farmers move silently along the pens, and all the day men and boys stand patiently in a line, holding their sheep for the judge's inspection. Then the crowd wanders up the hill to where the sheep-dog trials are being held. These are all local dogs—the owners themselves are never quite sure what they will do—but most obey every tone of their masters' voices; though this is different from work on the fells they rise to it, helping with infinite patience and intelligence to get the sheep through the hurdles. It is a difficult course, and in 1935, though many got their sheep through the last but one, known as the Maltese cross, only the Abbotside shepherd's dog finished the trial.

Paths branch down from Shaw Paddock to West End and Lunds on the other side of the river. The name Lunds comes from the Norse *lundr*, a wood. There is a town called Lund in Norway. Old documents give it as 'The Lundes,' and the dalespeople still use the prefix, and call it 'T' Lunds.' Up to the reign of Queen Elizabeth a Norse speech was used here, and Norse words linger; a barn is still a laithe. There is a feeling of agelessness about this district. It has the power of taking you to itself, so that you ask for nothing more.

D

The memory of those who have lived and struggled in it hangs over it, not oppressively, but because of necessity they were so much a part of it that they have left something of themselves here. Man has long ventured to dwell in it, but there is a certain defiance about the houses he has built.

These houses are plain and rough, made to stand the weather. There was little time or money to ornament them, though in a carthouse at West End there is a stone built into the inner wall with the inscription 'W. P., 1676.' A William Parkin mentioned in a tithe list for 1675 probably put this stone above the door of the house he built. A small ogee-headed window in another outhouse may have been brought from Pendragon Castle. This group of three houses, one now derelict, clustered about Washet Gill, is the only attempt in Lunds of gathering together. One daleswoman said: 'I'd not mind livin' there; it's snug an' quiet.'

Notable men have been connected with Lunds. In West End was born John Blades, who went to London in 1779 with half a crown in his pocket, and in 1813 was made Sheriff of London. It is believed that he walked down Ludgate Hill, and asked at the door of a house for a situation. He was given work as a porter, and finally married the daughter of the house and became owner of the business of cut and ornamental glass. He is buried in Lunds churchyard.

Place, the whitewashed farmhouse by the church, was once four livings, and was bought in 1874 by Thomas Hewitson, who founded the first large furniture shop in Tottenham Court Road, London. Shaws, the house above it, was for fourteen years the home of Mr. R. A. Scott Macfie, the editor of the *Gypsy Lore Journal*. He was much loved by the dalespeople. He made the road down to the church, and planted trees on each side of it, and put planks across the river and the beck where before they had to be forded. He died in 1935, and is buried in the churchyard.

In the midst of Lunds, a focus for the valley, stands the little church, 1,100 feet above sea-level, one of the simplest and remotest churches in England. But for its bell-cote you might mistake it for a barn. It stands in a tremendous churchyard where the few gravestones look lost. There is no porch; only the door and two circular - headed windows break the walls. William Howitt, on a visit in 1839, found the snow coming through the roof, and the bell broken, so that the sexton had to call the congregation by climbing up and shouting 'bol lol, bol lol!' through the hole, and the only door was a thorn-bush. Somewhere about this time, during the funeral service of a William Cleasby, who was reported to have been a very wicked man, there was such a heavy snowstorm that the coffin could not be squeezed into the grave. For two nights it had to be left in the church, and all the time a robin, flying in through the thorn-bush, perched on it, keeping guard.

Exactly when Lunds church was built is not known, but a curate was licensed to it in 1713, so it was probably started earlier in the seventeenth century, and built by the parishioners' own hands. Its rough walls are now so much a part of the countryside that they reflect its deep repose. The benefice was united with that of

Hardraw in 1858, and the vicar comes from Hardraw to a service every Sunday afternoon. Before that time Lunds had its own curate, but never a vicarage. The stipend was small, and most of the incumbents were readers or schoolmasters who regarded Lunds as a stepping-off place for higher honours in the church. It was always changing its curates—in twenty-eight years it had thirteen—and when it lost them it often lost its schoolmaster at the same time. One curate is said to have preached at Hardraw in the morning, Lunds in the afternoon, and Dent at night.

There are few to attend the church now, but they come for special occasions, and wend home afterwards in all directions. One harvest festival time we stayed after the congregation had gone. For a few minutes the little church in its great garth looked forsaken and forlorn. Wild Boar Fell seemed to shut out the world. On the hillside behind, meadows and moorland jutted into each other; Lunds Fell was the golden brown of autumn with patches of bracken here and there a deep bronze. Streaks of sunlight raced across it—it is strange how often when you see it from a distance Lunds is in a gleam of sun. The white farmhouse across the beck seemed to say: 'I 'm here,' and from the hill above, the other house, Shaws, looked down. A horse browsed near the church-yard, and there were cows. A man passed up the hill with his dog, driving sheep. And the church was lonely no longer, the life of the valley had closed round it again.

There is a tradition that before the church was built services were held on Course Haw, the hill near, and that people were called to them by the ringing of a bell or beating on an iron pan. There may have been a preaching cross here. On the summit are large stones and signs of an enclosure. The pastures round have names as lovely as the hill: Benty Rigg, Witherside, Cockley Mace, High Spouty Close, Calf Rigg, Knittles, Little Grains.

Above the houses and the church, connected with them by paths and tracks, runs the old road, known here as Streets, which seems to indicate that the Romans made or used it. It has come up from Mallerstang, over Thrang Bridge and Hell Gill Bridge, past High Hall, whose original name was more appropriately Highway House, above Shaws, to High Dike. This house, now a barn, was also an inn. By the end of the eighteenth century there was so much traffic along the road that highwaymen considered it worth their while to frequent it. It was handed down from one landlord to another that Nevison, or 'Swift Nicks,' often called at High Dike Inn, riding a grey horse, and that he was 'a very gentlemanly man.' It was probably he, not Dick Turpin, who took that leap over Hell Gill Beck. The inn was occupied in 1877. Memories cling round it of the travellers who stopped here to rest and gossip; you almost hear the clatter of their horses' hoofs, listen to their tales, see the packman spread out his wares. There are memories too of children who toiled up the hillside, for in a cottage attached to the inn an old lady kept a school, known as Lunds School.

At the end of the fourteenth century the timber for the castle of the Scropes at Bolton was brought along this road. In 1568 Mary Queen of Scots rode along it

on her way to imprisonment in the castle. In 1663
Anne Clifford, Countess of Dorset and Pembroke,
travelled it from Nappa Hall to her castle of Pendragon
beyond Hell Gill. She tells in her diary how she came
'over the Stake into Wensledale to my cousin Mr.
Thomas Metcalfe's house at Nappa, and the next day I
went over Cotter, which I lately repaired, and I came
into this Pendragon's Castle. And this was the first
time I was ever in Kettlewelldale, or went over Buckden
Rakes or Stake, or any of those dangerous places,
wherein yet God was pleased to preserve me in that
journey.'

The road was used chiefly by drovers and packmen.
Every year in October a horse fair was held at Brough
Hill in Westmorland, and on these days there was a
constant procession along it. The farmers' wives who
lived near the road would set out stalls with home-made
cakes and herb beer to sell. Brough Hill Fair still continues—though not many horses are sold now, it is a
great meeting-place for gipsies—but on those October
days the old road is as silent as on any others.

Immediately opposite to High Dike, a path, marked
now by shooting butts, runs across the moor to Cotterdale. It is said that the dead from Cotterdale, which
had no church, were brought along here to be buried
in the graveyard at Lunds. Across the fell lies Cotter
Tarn, where seagulls call over the still water. At its
edge we found the skull of a curlew with its long beak
perfect. Nothing else remained to tell how it, one of
the spirits of the moor, had died there.

The road runs along the ridge, following the wall for

much of the way. It is easy to find, but falls here and there into a narrow path, needing the repairs which Lady Anne Clifford gave it nearly three hundred years ago. Hers was the first four-wheeled carriage to go along the road; there are places now where a cart could not pass. When it was the main road it seemed to need frequent attention, for there are many entries in the book of the Constabulary of Bainbridge for 'repairing the Lunds road.' In a particularly deep shake-hole beside it a bird-cherry has rooted and grown into a large tree, its top no higher than the edge of the hollow. In that sheltered place it blooms as luxuriantly as if it were in the valley. Its branches and roots have spread across the hollow, and wool from sheep which have sheltered there clings to them.

At Cotter End the road plunges down the ridge and then is lost. Lady Anne Clifford's road went over Riggs Pasture, crossed the River Cotter above Cotter Force, turned up Pry House pastures, and skirted Fossdale to Simonstone. A later road went down from Cotter End to join the present main road just above Collier Holme Farm. Cotter End looks down the valley to which they lead, greener and more wooded than the one behind; from nowhere is there a better view of it. This walk along the old road is one of the finest walks in Yorkshire. Its position alone, on the high ridge, would make it that, and added to this is the memory which hangs over it of fuller, livelier days, of a life now gone in which it took a part.

So Lunds in this first wild stretch of Wensleydale is left. It remains in your mind as a piece of England where you can forget the noise and rush of modern life with its striving for things which here seem of no importance. A daleswoman of Lunds, giving her opinion of the country, said: 'Well, it's plain.' It is plain; here, where life is hard, nothing has come to spoil the country or the people.

Cotterdale

CHAPTER IV

MOSSDALE, WIDDALE FELL, AND COTTERDALE

THE road from the Moorcock Inn to Hawes is a main
road. Buses and cars come along it from Sedbergh and
the Lake District, but there is not an endless stream of
traffic, and for long periods of the year it is almost
deserted. It is an exhilarating road, with a free and easy
way of taking the hills, dipping here and there to get
fresh energy. Presently it crosses the Ure as a wide
highway over Mossdale Bridge, a modern, concrete
bridge, adequate for its purpose, but ugly. The old
Thwaite Bridge and curve of road which they replaced
are still there under the trees, seeming with the farmhouse which stands beside them to shrink back from

41

the wide road and all that it implies. Thwaite Bridge
is shown on Jeffrey's map of 1775.

A gate at the south end of the new bridge leads to
one of the smallest dales, Mossdale, which is little more
than the widening of the main valley. Its two farmhouses with whitewashed borders round the doors and
windows can be seen from further along the road. From
the distance they seem to be smiling, as if they were
delighted to peep from their valley at the outside world.
As we went over the hill to them we came across a
shepherd and a group of men busy 'crowning' the
Swaledale sheep. Each sheep was examined, and those
considered up to the standard were marked on the horn
ready for the sales at Hawes.

A small bridge crosses the beck between the farmhouses, and from it is seen the first of the two Mossdale
waterfalls, framed in an arch of the railway viaduct.
The second comes in a double fall over black, mossy
rocks at the end of the gorge. Trickles of water run
down the ravine; one has petrified the mosses and
branches in its course, and the rock and earth have a
polished appearance. This is a dreamy, aloof valley,
giving the feeling that no one has trodden it
or knows of it. It offers lazy hours beside its
stream, or it starts you out for the climb up Widdale
Fell.

Widdale Fell is perhaps the best placed of all the fells
grouped at the head of the dale above Hawes. There
are bolder hills, but it lies in the centre, and the view
from its summit is a panorama. As you rise there
appears on the lower slopes to the west another green

track, the old road from the head of Garsdale to Dentdale. The summit of Widdale Fell, called Great
Knoutberry Hill, is 2,203 feet high. The finest view-
point is at a place where two walls, coming up from the
south-east and the south-west, meet. Hills radiate in
all directions with nothing to hide them. You see the
dales which they enclose as far-off pictures slung between
the fells, in no way detracting from their wildness and
dignity; the narrow valley of Mallerstang; Grisedale
with its scattered, whitewashed farms; Garsdale; vivid
Dentdale, a wooded paradise; Ribblesdale; and eastwards
and nearer, part of Wensleydale. Between and beyond
them are the graver hills; the hills of Swaledale with
Micklefell and Warcop Fell beyond; Wild Boar Fell,
Swarth Fell, and Baugh Fell; Rise Hill, a network of
walls; the humpy Howgill Hills above Cautley. In the
distance are the misty mountains of the Lake District;
the well-known shapes of Whernside and Ingleborough;
across flatter country the isolated peak of Pendle Hill
in Lancashire; southwards the Wharfedale hills, Peny-
ghent, and the Whernsides; and eastwards the hills of
Lower Wensleydale and Swaledale. It is a little world
lying before you, a perfect circle, and you can work
round it again and again, and each time find some fresh
hill or corner of a valley.

Just below the summit on the east side are Widdale
Great Tarn and Widdale Little Tarn. Perhaps because
there are two of them, they have not the feeling of
desolation of most moorland tarns, but there is still the
melancholy lapping of the water against the sides. The
descent can be made over the fell into Widdale, along

the ridge and down to Appersett, or back on the other side of the stream to Mossdale.

Widdale is pronounced 'Widdel' in Wensleydale. Few of the places are pronounced as they are spelt. Mallerstang becomes 'Mauston'; Baugh Fell, 'Barfel'; Cragdale, 'Cregdel'; Cotterdale, 'Cotterdel'; and Mossdale, 'Mozdel,' and so on down the dale. The accent is invariably on the first syllable, and gives the names a lilt which makes the ordinary pronunciation sound stilted.

Cotterdale starts on the other side of the main road, a little lower down the valley than Mossdale. It can be reached from Cotter End, from Hardraw along East Side on Abbotside Common, or by the road which turns to it opposite Collier Holme Farm. This road has a good tarred surface, and yet it seems to be striking over the fells to nowhere—or it might be anywhere.

We came to Cotterdale first along the Hardraw track, which is on a ridge of the hill, and feels with every step to go deeper into its heart. We should have expected a valley there to be a desolate hollow, too remote and inaccessible for farms and habitation. Then we saw the hamlet in the rays of the setting sun. A beck ran through it; houses faced each other across a narrow road; smoke curled up from their chimneys; and there was a little chapel at the end where a gate shut it off from the fells. A small boy led a horse along the road and across the beck, and left it to graze; a woman shook a tablecloth through an open doorway. It was a scene of tranquillity; it seemed to belong to a time past, to be a ghostly village from another era. We climbed down the hillside to it, fearing to go round by the track lest it should vanish before we reached it. We should not have been surprised to find the people in the dress of hundreds of years ago.

The hamlet is as surprising when you get down to it. The Methodist chapel in its burial-ground and a shepherd's cottage in a garden beside it are at one end. Then beyond a little green the houses draw together, lining the road, and there is a sudden feeling of a narrow street in a town. These houses have a prosperous air, but round a bend there is a change. The cottages run only on one side of the road, and in between are ruins overgrown with nettles and trees. A sense of melancholy and desolation prevails, for derelict houses are more pathetic when they are together and lose the dignity of isolation. Then the ruins are past, and the village ends in a white cottage where a gamekeeper lives. In the other smaller dales of Wensleydale the farmhouses are scattered along the valley, surrounded by their meadows; this is the only one where they have gathered into a community. It is as though some cause far in the past made them draw together. Old documents refer to it as Cotterdale Town, and occasionally it gets that fitting name to-day. The name comes from a Norse word meaning 'hut' or 'cottage.'

On the south-east the village looks for a time down the valley to the meadows and pastures of the farms. Here the becks, East Gill and West Gill, flowing from the two ravines behind the village, join and become the River Cotter, which has a fine waterfall, Cotter Force, lower down its course. On all sides the fells overwrap the valley, and shut it in; there is no view of the bigger dale into which the river flows.

The almost secret position of the valley seems to have been taken advantage of in the sixteenth century. A survey taken by the Duke of Lennox about 1603 shows that six titled or wealthy men had small estates here, some with houses attached. It is strange to hear of so many such men grouped together in this remote place, but they were all descendants of men involved in Catholic plots in the early part of the reign of Queen Elizabeth, and their ancestors may have been given these holdings for a refuge in times of persecution. There was probably a cell here, for two of the tenants, Richard Leake and Leonard Lowther, were 'clarkes.' If they had wished to hide they could not have chosen a safer place.

To-day as deep a stillness must pervade it as when the Catholics used it as a sheltering place, perhaps an even greater one, for the ruined houses seem to add to the quietness. In the little burying-ground attached to the Methodist chapel there is a gravestone which has no name on it, only the words: 'We repose in peace here.' A Cotterdale man was asked why this had been left without a name.

'Whya,' he said, 'ther were no need to put a name, we all ken who they were.'

'Yes, but in fifty or sixty years when you are all gone, how will people know?'

'Why, what 'll it matter, anyway?' he replied.

Even to-day for wheeled traffic there is only one road which stops here. This ending of the road was the subject of a rhyme made when the three principal families in Cotterdale were the Halls, Kirks, and Kings.

> Three halls, two kirks, and a king,
> Same road out as goes in.

In the nineteenth century this rhyme was used to settle a dispute about a right of way. From time immemorial the people of Cotterdale had used a path from the head of the dale over the lower slopes of Shunnor Fell to Thwaite in Swaledale. A new landlord declared the path closed, but the people went on using it. The case was taken to London, and one of the witnesses was an old man from Cotterdale. He told how he went that way every year to Thwaite Fair and, asked if he always kept to the same track, said: 'Aye, as near as a toucher.' He was asked to repeat the rhyme, and it decided the case against them, for it was declared that if there was only one way in and out there could be no right of way over the fell.

Tracks led up the moor to Cotterdale coal-pits, a mile away. This industry, which had brought more people into the village, declined with modern transport, and the houses of the workers became the ruins you see. Old people remember thirty 'livings' in Cotterdale. Beside those in the village, there were seven on the road and by the sides of the beck where now there are none. A few generations ago in one of these, called Woodclose, which was across the beck some distance from the village, a fire of moor coal was kept burning night and day. If it happened to go out the occupants came as far as the village, and a burning peat was thrown across to them.

The people were poor, and made a little extra money by knitting. A Betty Slinger, living in Cotterdale a hundred years ago, used to walk to Hawes every market-day with her week's knitting in a bundle on her head, knitting on both journeys, and while she did her shopping, and often completing in the day a pair of men's stockings. When knitting was no longer an industry the habit of it clung here. Some time in the eighteen-nineties a young woman went with her husband to live in Cotterdale. They were not welcomed very well, because neither of them belonged to the dale. The women, who were all older than she, could not forgive this new-comer because she did not knit.

'Why,' said one woman, 'I knits a sock under t' blankets every neet after I 've gaen to bed.'

But the new-comer was equal to her. 'It seems to me,' she said, 'ye 'll not be savin' much that way. Ye 'll soon wear out t' blankets.'

Some of the reserve and sufficiency of the valley seems to have grown into the people. They appear suspicious of strangers, but underneath their shyness and reserve there is all the dale humour and friendliness unspoilt.

The first time we went to Cotterdale we saw reared up against the wall at the side of the road an octagonal stone bowl, very like a font. We wondered about it. Had it come from the Catholic cell, or was it a font at all? The next time we went the font had gone, and we stared unbelieving at the empty wall. Cotterdale had its usual forsaken air, but presently two little boys peeped round a corner.

'What has happened to the stone bowl which used to be here?' we asked.

They looked hard at us, then one of them said: 'I deean't knaw.'

We all stood and looked at the wall for a long time, till the other boy spoke. 'It's i' t' pigsty,' he said.

They opened the door of the pigsty, and there beside a larger stone trough stood the font, with a rim of pig food round its edge. The farmer kept two pigs and, one always being greedier than the other, the font was brought in so that each had his own bowl. Years of rolling in and out of the pigsty had rounded its edges.

Then the farmer and his sister appeared, and we explained that we had come to look at the font.

'Nay, my good women,' said the sister, 'it's nivver a font, it's a pig trough.'

Her brother said nothing, but quietly walked to the other side of the road, pulled some stones off the end of a wall, and displayed another font-like bowl. We gazed in astonishment, confronted with not one but two fonts. The second font had a piece out of one side, but this, we were told, had been thrown into the beck during a flood.

By this time half the village had gathered round, and there was an eager group of children, with the fair hair of the dales children conspicuous. An old lady remembered that in the knitting days the first font was used for soaking the completed stockings to shrink them, and was known as the 'wash-bowl.' The next day we came with two other interested people, bringing with us a serviceable but unlovely pig trough to exchange for the

K

font, which was taken to Askrigg for more light to be thrown on its history.

Sixty years ago a little boy was the only child going to school from Cotterdale. There were one or two girls of school age, but their parents did not trouble to send them, so he had to walk the three miles to Hardraw alone. There was then no post box in the village, and as he was often the only person going out of it, on his way home he used to collect the letters, which were left in a wooden box where the road joins the main road. To-day quite a crowd of children make the journey to Hardraw to school, but have only to walk to the road end, where they are met by a governess car, in which, packed tightly with the driver towering above them, they remind you of the old woman and her family in the shoe.

Behind Cotterdale the two ravines of East and West Gill cut their melancholy way into the fell. The Ordnance Survey map of 1852 gives a John-o'-Groat's House high up on West Gill, and Cotterdale House, which is a cave, in East Gill.

The road out crosses West Gill by a bridge, and goes lonely and deserted along the slope of the fell. The map of 1852 gives a Dunne Bottom House in a field still known as Dunne Bottom on the lower side. This is now a barn. There is also a Nanny Dunne Well, and a Nanny Dunne Table, which may be a mound in the field. The well is supposed to be haunted by a woman with no head. It was probably given the name Nanny in the days when witches were believed in —Nanny was a common name for a witch, and had its origin in pagan days. It is known that there were early settlers in Cotterdale, for an Iron Age sword dating from about A.D. 50, and now in the British Museum, was found here. Strange things too have been seen. One night a man saw a figure with the body of a goat and the head and shoulders of a man leap the wall on to the main road near the River Cotter, cross the road, and disappear over the other side.

Presently the road from Cotterdale, striking over the fell, goes through a gate, and the village is lost behind the hill. Leaving it is like closing the last page of a book which has kept your interest to the end.

Appersett

CHAPTER V

APPERSETT, WIDDALE, AND SNAIZEHOLME

AFTER the River Ure has been joined by the Cotter, the road runs beside it for a time. Trees line it, and its sylvan beauty seems to belong to a softer country. Then the road forks, one way going north and one south of the river, beginning the two routes down the valley. The main road curves to the right to cross the Ure, and almost immediately turns sharply over another bridge across Widdale Beck. Below it, as though it had slid there, lies Appersett, the first village in Wensleydale.

The view of Appersett from this side is of slopes of cottage roofs, rising in tiers from the road, their stone darkened by the years, and coloured in places with moss and lichen. It has a look of gnarled age, like a bent old man whose life has been a struggle. Across the road is a green, bordered on one side by Widdale Beck. Like most Wensleydale villages, Appersett lies, not on the Ure, but on a beck which is just about to enter it. From the green you see the meeting lower down the valley, where the Ure runs its uncompanioned way. Widdale Beck threads a burbling course through a stony bed which looks much too wide for it, but at times it rises over the green and the road, and enters some of the houses.

Most of the houses turn their backs to the road and the green, as if they were running away, and face another street, called Brantome, and more houses. On this side they have a friendlier air than the one they turn to the road. Here are the people, and here is the reason why Appersett often looks deserted as you pass through.

The village ends at the east in a small meadow which might be any walled-in field, but for one tombstone. This commemorates a man and his wife who once lived at High Shaw Paddock in Lunds. They were Sandemanians, who did not wish to be buried in consecrated ground, and had the field prepared while they were still alive. From this end Appersett appears in another aspect. It seems to huddle under the slopes of Widdale Fell, which crouches over it like a great beast keeping guard.

The houses may turn away, but the real heart of Appersett is the green. Flocks of geese and goslings, and often cows or a horse, graze on it; children play about it, the girls in one group and the boys in another, as is the habit of country children; on washing days the women emerge from the houses with baskets full of clothes, and decorate it with all shapes and colours;

they come too with their piles of rubbish, ashes and tins, to the bank of the beck. There is nothing neat about the green; it is very much as you imagine it was when Appersett first became a village. It remains what a village green was meant to be, a piece of common land for the use of the villagers.

The name Appersett comes from the Old English, and means the 'shieling by the apple tree.' There are no apple trees now, nor does it give the impression of such settled things as orchards. It belongs more to the open spaces which are all around it, and the roads which lead to them. It has a gipsy quality, as if it were camping beside this green and beck, and might at some whim move on to another site. The road turning over the bridge calls to adventure and the joy of freedom.

Perhaps because they find themselves in sympathy with the elusiveness of the village, a family of gipsies has settled here. The father, like many of the gipsies, was a horse dealer, and used to go round to the fairs selling horses. Since he died his wife has made a living as a potter, and is well known down the dale. They have broken away from some of the habits of gipsies, living in the house in Appersett all the year round, but they have their dignity and quiet acceptance of whatever life brings. Their gipsy relations and friends come and visit them in intervals between fairs. Caravans rest in the space at the end of the houses, and there is often a tent in a field below the bridge with a gipsy cart tipped up beside it. The village seems to open its arms to receive them, as if for it the climax of the year had come.

Gipsies and potters frequent the Wensleydale roads,

coming to the small fairs which survive in the dale, and journeying to and from the big Westmorland fairs of Appleby and Brough Hill. Sometimes they camp on one of the green tracks, and depart, leaving only the burnt circle where their fires have been to tell of their stay. They sell their baskets and pots in the villages they pass through, and as the time for their visits **draws near** the people look for their coming.

A narrow road runs up Appersett Ghyll, beside Widdale Beck, joining in a mile and a half the main road from Hawes to Ingleton up Widdale. Where the roads meet, there used to be a toll house called Catch-penny House. It was kept for many years by an old woman who could not read. She knew the ordinary tolls, but not all that was on the paper which the turn-pike company delivered, and it worried her that she might be missing something. She was not anxious to display her ignorance, and as one of the Widdale farmers had sent his son to a school in Hawes, she waited until the boy had learnt to read, and one day stopped him on his way home.

'John,' she said, 'I want ye to read everything to me that's on that paper.'

The boy began, and she was pleased to find that for one particular kind of vehicle she could ask a penny more.

Then he came to a part which said that carts going and coming for coals were not to pay toll, and she had been charging for these.

'Nay, lad,' said the old woman, 'that'll do, tha mun read na further.'

She made an arrangement with the boy's father that

all his carts should go through toll free if he would not tell any one.

Widdale is a wild dale. Although its name shows that it was once wooded, it seems to belong now to the fells. You can imagine it without the strip of pasture and meadow round the beck, or the few dotted farms, each with its group of trees to protect it from the wind. The road swings upwards to the open moor with the farmhouses below, past the little schoolhouse, no longer used as a school, by the road which leads to Snaizeholme, through the boundary of the North and West Riding, till it comes to Newby Head, and a vast stretch of moorland. The house at Newby Head was until recently an inn. Drovers put up there on their way to the fairs, and thousands of sheep, cattle, and horses would be gathered outside.

A road beyond Newby Head turns down to Dentdale. This was made in 1802, when the Constabulary of Bainbridge gave fifty pounds towards its cost to the township of Dent, and it was agreed that the Dent road which ran along Widdale Fell should no longer be repaired. The old road which branches off opposite the schoolhouse can still be followed.

The dale of Snaizeholme runs into Widdale. Tracks lead up to it, one from near Catchpenny, another following the beck, and another by the schoolhouse, none giving any hint of the snug valley to which they are going. It can also be entered by a grassy, walled lane, which turns from the Widdale road a mile above Hawes. This is called the Cam High Road, and, until the turnpike road was made up Widdale, was the main road to

Ribble Head and the west. It cuts over the fells almost
to the summits of Ten End and Dodd Fell, beyond which
it joins the Roman road from Bainbridge.

We turned up this green lane one day in May. The
night before there had been a heavy snowstorm, and
snow still lay in the ridges of the hills and under the
scars. But it was a vain endeavour of winter's to return,
and now, as if it realized that it had been dallying, spring
had come in full force; already the snow looked unreal
in the hot sun. We went slowly. A plover screeched
over us angrily, and we stopped for a sight of its fluffy
brown babies, but the plover is an adept in the art of
deception. At the roadside was a barn, the lower part
of which had been made for a cowshed with slabs of solid
stone to divide the stalls. The cows were not yet in the
fields, but there was no sign of its having been used, and
it emphasized the desertion of the road.

Far ahead of us at the top of a long rise a man crossed
the fell with his dog. He stood for a moment, and looked
down towards us, and he and the dog, silhouetted against
the sky, seemed an immense distance away. As we
climbed, farmhouses appeared on the other side of the
valley which we knew was there. Then we saw the
farmer again, rounding sheep in a field, and he waited
for us to come up. We asked him where the grassy
road went.

'It gaes to Horton-i'-Ribblesdil,' he said, 'but ye 'll
git thar to-morn at neet at t' rate ye 're gaen.'

We said we did not want to go to Horton-in-Ribblesdale, but to Snaizeholme, and was there a way down
through his field?

'Nay, ther 's neea way through here.'

We none of us moved. We knew this was not a dismissal, and in a minute he began to open the gate deliberately.

'I 'll let ye through,' he said, 'an' than ye can ho'd yon sheep for me while I git t' other tweea oot. They 're nut mine, they 've gitten ower t' wall. An' than I 'll tak ye doon an' show ye t' rooad.'

So we went through the gate and, with strict instructions not to let go whatever it did, we each held a horn of the sheep which was in its right field, and the farmer and his dog turned out the trespassing ones, and then went down the hill with us. At the bottom of the field we came to High Houses and the path which runs along the east side of Snaizeholme, and our guide pointed out the way to the head of the valley.

'Noo, ye gan on this trod 'ere to whare ye see yon reek—ther 's a hoose below t' hill—than up ower yon meadow—ye can see t' path through t' muck—till ye come to t' beck; ye 'll finnd a brig thar which is nowt but a girt steean flag wi' railin's—ye 'll nut miss it, because it 's meeade o' a lump o' steean five yeeards lang. Than ye gan up by a leeathe (barn), an' into that meadow whar ye see 'em 'arrowin' muck. Efter that ther 's a good trod reight to t' end wi' stiles all t' way.' He turned to go. 'Noo, that 'll land ye reight eneuf, an' when ye cu back ye 'll 'a' been as oft as I 'ev.'

All the essentials of Snaizeholme were in that description. Farmhouses, smoke from their chimneys; little bridges over becks; barns; stiles made narrow so that the sheep cannot get through; meadows, and men

spreading manure on them; farmers, who, except to go
to market, move little from their own homes.

At a lower farm a goose and gander were grazing with
a family of yellow goslings. They moved away with
a walk which was almost a sail, and a look which
was a mixture of dignity and scorn. The goslings
followed, hurriedly nibbling the grass as they went.
Geese are a familiar sight in Upper Wensleydale, cropping
the grass with a tearing sound, basking in the sun, and
flying low if startled. But in proportion to its size,
there seem the greatest number in Snaizeholme, although
a farmer said that 'Gayle is a terrible spot for geese.'
Nowadays the goslings are sold when they are three or
four weeks old, but when more geese were kept the
farmer who had enough land to graze them would keep
his flocks until they were fully grown, and then take
them to Northallerton market. In still earlier days,
when the geese had to be driven by road, this was a
long and tedious journey. Except when they are being
fattened for market, the geese feed solely on grass and,
like the sheep and lambs, are turned higher on to the
fells as the meadows are needed for hay. Each farm, and
often each cottage in the hamlets, had so many goose
gaits on the moor, but many cottagers have either sold
their goose gaits, or not claimed them for many years.
On stinted land two geese correspond to one sheep.

During the nineteenth century goose parties were a
favourite form of entertainment in Snaizeholme. These
were given in the week between Christmas and New
Year's Day, and were attended only by the men. Whist
was played all evening, and the man at whose house the

party was held would give a goose as a prize, the winner
of which invited them all back to his house the next
night to play whist and eat the goose. He in his turn
gave another goose for the prize, and the winner had to
hold the party the next night, and so it went on until
New Year's Day.

We found the stone flag bridge, and the banks of the
beck near it were thick with primroses and violets in
full bloom, and bluebells just beginning to show their
buds. Across the meadows where the dark piles of
'muck' were being scattered into a thin layer, we came
to a farm which has the fitting name of Cow Hill.

There was an unusual group in a corner made by the
buildings. The farmer sat on a stool, holding between
his knees a sheep whose broken leg he was setting. His
two small sons watched intently, and the sheep looked
out with terror in her beady eyes. When the splint was
in place she was let go again, to remain in the meadow
for the night with her lamb to get used to it.

Then one of the little boys brought out from the barn
a tiny lamb, which followed him wherever he went,
running in jerky leaps. He had insisted on its being
branded with the other lambs, and it had a blue letter M
almost as big as itself on its back. It had no more fear
of human beings than a puppy. When it was born it
was small enough to fit into the child's Wellington boot,
and even now it was like a toy come to life. These
pet lambs are a nuisance when they grow up; they will
make their way back to the farmhouse whenever they
can, enticing more sheep with them.

From the head of the valley we looked back at it. It

was beautiful in the bright light, the sky a brilliant blue, banked with heavy white clouds. The fells, still lightened with snow, rolled down to embrace the scattered farmhouses, which were dark patches amongst the new green of the grass and trees. Only a few fields divided them, so that they did not look lonely, but each was different, and had its own character.

There are plantations of trees along the hillsides; ashes, elms, elders, and clumps of pine trees. The name Snaizeholme comes from the Old Norse *sneis*, a twig. Its trees still provide firewood for the people.

In 1423 three men of Snaizeholme made a raid on the cattle of the monks of Jervaulx on Abbotside Common. Fourscore bullocks, valued at forty pounds, were taken. They were probably a wild people at that period, but as early as 1713 you find a 'John Allen of Snaizholm' presenting to Hawes church 'as a free gift from his sister, Mrs. Alēs Allen,' a silver communion cup of thirteen and a half ounces.

The road on the west side goes back along the ridge, but we followed a path beside the beck. As we dropped down to it the sun seemed to burn intensely, its rays showing through the clouds. 'It's a thunder sun,' said a farmer, coming down to milk his cows; 'there'll be thunder and rain soon.'

The farmer told us how he had looked out from his house early that morning, and seen the valley and the trees in full leaf lying thick with snow.

'I thought to myself,' he said, 'that I'd never seen anything so beautiful.'

It was surprising to find a dalesman praising his own

dale. He is generally proud of it, but slow to say so. 'Aye, it's all reight i' summer,' is his usual remark to others' praise.

A group of ducks, their snowy feathers dazzling in their purity, swam down the beck in front of us, paddling placidly through the pools, and treading clumsily where it broke into miniature rapids. Beyond the last farm we followed the road over the fell, and when we turned round again, the 'valley of the twigs' had disappeared, and we were back in the wildness of Widdale.

Gayle

CHAPTER VI

GAYLE

GAYLE has the qualities which make for quaintness: hills rising above it, houses grouped round the beck, narrow alleys, a bridge, a mill, each so perfectly placed that a first view is startling. It lies only a mile from Hawes, nearer by a short cut across the fields. The two places practically merge into each other, but they present a contrast—Hawes, new and growing; Gayle, old and standing still, as if a spell had been laid upon it. It is to be hoped that the spell will not be lifted, for Gayle could not be replaced.

The village lies at the foot of Sleddale, clustering round the Duerley Beck, and sheltering under Ten End and Dodd Fell. The beck is the heart of Gayle. It has determined its plan. Its bed of solid rock at one place forms a shelf, making a waterfall, and when the water is low the people cross along the top of the shelf instead of going round to the bridge. Children walk unconcernedly across; old women pick their way gingerly; horses and cattle come to the beck to drink; muddy coats are brought to be rinsed, or you see a motor lorry standing in the middle getting its weekly wash. It is open to the road on one side, as if it realized its usefulness.

The houses cluster about the beck, and the narrow, cobbled alleys dividing them have quaint names like Marridales, Beckstones, Wynd, Hargill, Garris, Gaits, Thundering Lane. Some of the houses whose elaborate doorways have dates and initials were built by such families as the Whaleys, Metcalfes, or Rouths, one of whom was chief forester of Wensleydale in the fourteenth century; but these are now farmhouses.

A stone bridge crosses the beck, and here in the evening, when the day's work is done, the men come and stand. To stay long in Gayle is to find yourself drifting towards the bridge, leaning on its wall, and gazing at the beck. You may think sometimes of the places to which the water is going, jostling down the green dale till it reaches the city of Ripon, through rolling country to York, winding along flatter land to the port of Hull, till it waves a good-bye for ever at Spurn Head. But you will not often get so far; when you are in a Yorkshire dale any country beyond seems of little count. And Gayle itself is sufficient to think of—Gayle to-day and Gayle yesterday.

Looking towards Hawes is the mill which was

advertised 'To Let' in 1844 as 'containing three large
rooms, and a special garret; this mill has been used
for the several purposes of Cotton, Flax, and Wool
spinning.' To-day it is a saw-mill, cutting mostly local
timber for gates and fences.

Beyond the mill the tower of Hawes church with its
'pepper-pot' turret shows above the ridge which hides
most of the town. These two places so near to each other
cherished for a long period a bitter feud. How it started
is not known; perhaps it originated in the days of the
Celts and Norsemen. The slogan of Gayle was: 'Aye,
aye, for t' Gayle,' and the Hawes men would reply:
'Yo' can shute, but yo' can't buy owt i' Gayle'; a retort
which they could not make with truth to-day, for there
are several shops. There is a story of a Hawes man who
was proud to possess the nickname of 'The Mayor of
Hawes.' One night at an inn in the town he was
boasting, and challenged any one to a fight. A Gayle
man coming in heard the challenge, and went up to him
and said: 'If thee 's t' mayor o' t' Haas, I 'm t' hoss o'
Gayle,' a remark which sobered the Hawes 'mayor.'
Not until after the Great War did the feud die. Men
came home with different ideas; they had made friends
outside, and could understand the rest of the world better.

The village hall on the Burtersett road was once a
Sandemanian chapel. This was one of many religions
which broke away from the Wesleyan church, usually to
follow one man who gave his name to the sect, like the
'Barkerites' and 'Grahamites'; 'fancy religions,' a daleswoman called them. The Sandemanians, founded by
Robert Sandeman and John Glas, had a great following

F

in the dale for a time. Occasional burials still take place in the burial - ground, whose tombstones show the dissenting families of the district from the end of the eighteenth century, chiefly Allens and Dinsdales. A building just below the bridge was known as the 'mess house,' because the people who came to the chapel from long distances had their meals there, and also stabled their horses, for many of them arrived in carts.

From the other side of the beck you see the cottages of the village. Gayle was chiefly a place of cottages with smallholdings, their tenants being generally wallers or drainers, who worked on the farms of the district. To-day these employments do not provide a living; few walls are being built, and the farmer himself repairs the old ones as they fall, and does any necessary draining. The land is suffering now from the lack of more extensive draining.

These cottagers were desperately poor. Often the drainers were forced to do their work by contract, and for such a small sum that they had to work every hour of daylight to make anything out of it. They had no time to stop for meals; they would place their oatcake along the side of the drain, and take a bite as they went along. Their food was of the plainest, chiefly oatcake and cheese, seldom bread. Meat was a luxury. It was said in those days that if a cow or sheep died it was not buried, but was sent to Gayle. Each cottager kept a goose, and these were often allowed to sleep in the kitchen, where a box was left for them. In spring they would come in to lay, and later would sit and hatch out the eggs there.

Gayle of all places in Wensleydale has been most known
for its knitters, possibly because the industry survived
longest here. Men, women, and children knitted in
their spare time; old people who were no longer able to
do other work earned something towards their keep by it.

The industry goes back to the middle of the sixteenth
century, when knitting schools were started to teach
poor children how to knit. These were particularly
successful in the dales. By the end of the century
'14 or 16 packes, each with 40 dossen pare of stockings,'
were taken to Richmond market every week. Kendal
was another market. Knitted stockings were amongst
the articles seized as payment for tithes from the
Quakers. Towards the end of the seventeenth century
Edmond Fothergill had four dozen stockings taken,
valued at twenty-eight shillings. A pair of coarse wool
stockings could be bought for eightpence halfpenny at
the end of the eighteenth century.

At first the knitting was done with wool from local
sheep, spun in the cottages. But as bigger quantities
were required the yarn was bought, usually from hosiers
who travelled round the smaller markets selling yarn
and buying back the completed garments, stockings,
gloves, caps, jerseys, etc. The yarn was very coarse, and
was known as 'bump.' As machinery came in, mills
were opened for spinning yarn, and the owner of the mill
took the place of the hosier. Hawes mill employed
four hundred knitters in their own homes, and from
fifteen to twenty in the mill. By the end of the nineteenth century machinery had killed the hand-knitting
industry.

The work was very poorly paid, a few pence for a pair of stockings which came nearly to the thigh—the wool was unshrunk, and the garments had to be made big enough to allow for shrinking afterwards. Some of the mill-owners, who were often landowners as well, ground down the people. One woman in Gayle, who knitted incessantly for food and clothing for her children, was told when she went for a new supply of yarn that she would receive less for her next week's knitting. She was a typical daleswoman, strong willed and independent, and she was not afraid to tell the mill-owner what she thought of him. When she was an old woman over ninety—'old Moll' she was always called in the village —she loved to relate how she 'just steud up to him, and said: "We've drained ye yer land, do ye want us to lime it an' all?"'

Women knitted as they moved about the house, children as they learnt their lessons in school, men as they drove their carts along the road, shepherded the sheep, or walked to the lead and coal mines; and in the evening, when their other work was done, they knitted harder than ever. It was drudgery, but it must have been picturesque drudgery, and they made the best of it. To save fuel they would meet in turn at each other's houses, and sit round the fire, talking as they knitted. Sometimes one of them read from a book like *Pilgrim's Progress*; sometimes they sang; or they passed the time by knitting a row for each house in the village, starting at one end and seeing who got round first. But the favourite entertainment was telling ghost stories. When these were particularly thrilling the hostess would say:

'We 'll not part to-night,' and fling another peat on the fire, and they would sit on until midnight, by which time they were almost too terrified to go home. They called these meetings 'goin' a-sittin'.' Their illumination was the light of the fire; if a knitter dropped a stitch she would call out: 'Turn the peat,' and the fire was poked to make a glow. Sometimes a candle was lit for a dropped stitch, but it was blown out immediately.

They knitted with curved needles with a peculiar swaying movement, and the needle from which the stitches were being taken was pushed into a wooden sheath, worn tucked into a belt. These sheaths were treasured possessions; they are made of wood, often plum wood, and shaped like a goose wing; some are beautifully carved and inlaid with mother-of-pearl. A young man's favourite present for his sweetheart was a sheath which he had carved himself. An old lady lower down the dale remembers when she was five years old walking down the village street, when a donkey came clattering along, ridden by a boy a little older than she, who shouted: 'I 'll run ye down, I 'll run ye down.' Terrified, she ran into a cottage, and the old man who lived there gave her a knitting sheath to comfort her. She has it yet. It is a special treasure, because when she grew up she married the boy who rode the donkey. The sheaths and knitting needles are heirlooms now, and the chances are that you will not see a knitter as you stand on the bridge at Gayle.

As you watch, the ease and placidity of the village lay hold of you. You take the place to your heart, but you must not imagine that it has done the same to you.

Gayle is a difficult place to get inside, unless your family belongs. This suspicion of strangers, characteristic of all the remote parts of the Yorkshire dales, probably has its roots far back in the days of invasions and raids. It seemed to reach its height in Gayle. Here the 'foreigner' was not necessarily from far away, but any one who had not been born and brought up in the village. They even resented one of their men bringing a wife from another part. It would take this wife most of her married life, always behaving tactfully, to be accepted as one of them. As a result the people have intermarried, and so many have the same name that nicknames are used, and often their real names are forgotten. A stranger once came into Gayle and asked for Mr. John Dinsdale, but nobody could tell who he was or where he lived. Then his nickname, Brassy Jack, was mentioned, and everybody knew.

The habit of using by-names has probably descended from the Viking settlers, who are known to have been fond of them. Sometimes a man is called by his trade, as John o' t' Post (pronounced 'Posst'), Butcher Tom, Cobber Dickey; or some characteristic is taken, as Brassy Doad, Kit Moss; or the name of their farm is added, as Geordie Horrabank. The name Peacock is often turned into 'Puke.' And there is the usual dale habit of calling a man after his father or mother, as Kit Tom, Bella Jimmy, Betty Ned. Other names are Jappa, Shappa, Romma, Nelse, Rannock. Rannock is sometimes applied to Swaledale men.

A little way out of the village, at the east end, near Blackburn Farm, there are the remains of an ancient camp, a square platform, now cut by the road, with signs of a ditch on the north and east sides. From the days when it was made there has been life on this ridge overlooking the valley.

Straight out of Gayle there starts that romantic pass which runs over Fleet Moss into Langstrothdale, the head of Wharfedale, and is known as Greensett. Far past all houses it crosses the Roman road from Bainbridge, and runs out of sight of cultivation until farms and the clustered cottages of Oughtershaw appear, and another dale starts.

At Scar Head a path runs down to Duerley Beck—Sleddale does not take its name from the beck. A dalesman remembers thirty or forty years ago camping near the farmhouse of Duerley Bottom. The old lady at the farm saw the tent, and said: 'Tha's nivver gaen to sleep under yon lump o' clout?' She would be amazed to see the 'lumps o' clout' in Wensleydale at holiday times now.

Aisgill Falls on Duerley Beck drop thirty feet over rock which curves outwards like a dome, and are awe-inspiring when the beck is full. A path runs beside the beck to Gayle, and there is a track over the fell, passing near a lonely farm called Gaudy. A field's length from the house here a little vegetable and fruit garden has been made, and as we passed, a goose sitting on a nest in a corner of it peered out at us.

From this side of Sleddale you see the Greensett road striking courageously up Fleet Moss. Below, the edge of Ten End merges gradually from brown fell to green pasture; Gayle seems to curve round the tip of it.

Beyond, is Wensleydale again, its walls gleaming white against the fields in the sun. The river is hidden, but a train going slowly up the dale leaves a trail of smoke. There are the villages, Hardraw, Sedbusk, Askrigg, and farmhouses dotting the spaces between. Into its graciousness the Sleddale valley turns, and unconsciously you quicken your footsteps to follow it. A flagged path beyond the village leads from Gayle into Hawes, that centre of the upper dale.

CHAPTER VII

HARDRAW, FOSSDALE, AND SEDBUSK

HAWES and Hardraw, facing each other across the river, go different ways. Hardraw, on the north side of the valley, begins the long line of villages which rest at the foot of the fells, and seem to belong to them. It lies snugly under Abbotside Common on the lower slopes of Shunnor Fell, which, though the highest hill in Wensleydale, rolls backwards, and does not dominate the valley as do some of the lesser hills. It is a tiny village. There is no shop, but it has its own church and school, and a proper country inn, the 'Green Dragon.' Many of the houses are new, and the church was rebuilt in 1880 by the Earl of Wharncliffe. Beyond the bridge which crosses the beck a Tudor hall, now a farmhouse,

73

remains. Its paved court has been walled to form a yard and sheep-folds.

We have watched the farmer and his sons clipping sheep in a small grassy enclosure here, the farmer sitting on a bench called a 'sheep cratch.' As each sheep was shorn it was marked with blue paint, and taken back, looking naked and ungainly without its wool. There were occasional interruptions to rub ointment on a slight cut or scratch, and to roll the fleeces ready for storing. The harvesting of the wool seems necessarily a leisurely proceeding, but a good shearer will clip ten sheep in an hour.

The name Hardraw comes from the Old English, and means 'the shepherd's dwelling.' There is still a shepherd's dwelling here, occupied by one of the four shepherds of Abbotside.

Abbotside Common, which, under the names of High and Low Abbotside, stretches on the north side of the valley from Hell Gill to Skellgill, near Askrigg, received its name from the fact that it formed part of the estate of Jervaulx Abbey. At the Dissolution it was given by Henry VIII to Matthew, Earl of Lennox, from whom it descended to James I. He granted it to Ludovick Stewart, Duke of Lennox and Richmond, who had great difficulty in getting the tenants to accept him. In 1603 Ludovick had a survey of Abbotside made because the rents of the farms were too low, and by it he found that he was only getting £100 where he should have been getting £1,200. Later he sold the estate to three men, one of them John Coleby, and after several changes High Abbotside descended to Lord Wharncliffe, who sold it in

1912. Its new owners divided this section, and sold the shooting rights, since when the number of sheep on the moor has been reduced. Abbotside was first stinted, that is the number of sheep were limited, in 1837.

Farmers on Abbotside Common are not allowed to do their own shepherding, but must pay a share towards the four shepherds employed. When a vacancy occurs a new shepherd is elected by a group of landowners, called the Conservators; at times there have been eighty applicants. The shepherds live at Lunds, Cotterdale, Hardraw, and Simonstone, and each one is responsible for about a thousand sheep; those in the care of the Hardraw shepherd belong to nine farmers. They are 'heughed' sheep, that is, sheep bred on the moor and which do not stray far from the area in which they grazed with their mothers. 'Heughed' sheep are often left on the farm when it changes hands, so that a new tenant comes to a flock which knows the moor. Each lot is easily recognized by the mark, which is a help to the shepherd when counting them. Only at special times, such as bringing them down for dipping, does the farmer assist with the sheep on the moor.

During unexpected snow-storms many sheep are buried by drifts while sheltering in hollows or under walls. Sometimes the shepherd finds them by walking along the wall and prodding his stick into the drifts, but the dogs are the greatest help, being able to scent them under the snow. They are often alive after being buried three weeks, and one sheep here lived seven weeks under a drift. They eat the grass, and often the earth, in the space which has melted round them, and some eat their

own wool. In searching for them the shepherd, knowing
the moor, is not afraid of hidden gullies and holes, but
he dislikes it when it is 'stowering,' that is, a bitterly
cold wind blowing the snow into his face, and almost
taking away his breath.

Behind the village, in Hardraw Scar, is the famous
waterfall, Hardraw Force, which, nearly a hundred feet
in height, is an impressive sight. It is in a ravine,
reached from the back of the inn by a path which
continues behind the falls, and on which it is possible
to walk without getting wet. The lower rock is soft
and shaly, easily worn away by water, and the limestone
rock projects at the top. At long intervals the ridge has
broken off, carrying on through thousands of years the
process of pushing back the ravine; it is now built up to
preserve it. There is a cave under the fall, and a tale is
told of a dog which went into it, and disappeared to
emerge at Cotterdale House Cave, above Cotterdale,
completely without hair.

Occasionally disastrous floods have swept down the
ravine. One of the worst remembered was in 1899
when there was a cloud-burst on Shunnor Fell, and
volumes of water, bringing tons of mud, rushed into the
village. The graveyard was practically washed away;
some tombstones were found three miles down the
valley, others were never recovered. A large tree fell
against the inn wall, and the table in the kitchen floated
up to the ceiling. In the next cottage a valuable old
tea service, of which the owner was very proud, floated
about the room, but when the flood subsided it was
found that only one saucer was broken.

In the winters of 1739 and 1881 Hardraw Force, along with others in Wensleydale, was frozen from top to bottom, making a hollow tube of ice. Any such unusual occurrence was generally made the opportunity for a concert. It was music which enhanced the fame of Hardraw. The sheltered ravine was found to have remarkable acoustic properties, and about 1885 several gentlemen in Hawes organized a band contest there. This was so successful that it became an annual event. Famous bands came from long distances to compete; Besses o' th' Barn and the Black Dyke bands won some of their first prizes, and are said to have made their names at these contests. Thousands of people came to Hardraw that day, and trains filled the line from Askrigg to Hawes Junction. Wagonettes charged sixpence to take people from Hawes station, and because of the crowds on the road had to return by Appersett. Sometimes there was not a crumb of food left in Hardraw or Hawes at the end of the day.

Later, competitions for choirs were added. These were held in a field on the top of the scar; the choirs and bands performed together, but neither could hear the other. Wooden seats were built round the bandstand, and winding paths made up the hillside, those winding paths with railings at the steep parts without which Victorians did not seem able to enjoy the country. Once a lady in a pale grey dress fell in the stream when trying to cross by the stepping-stones. Her choir was the next to compete, so there was no time to get dry, and as she stood singing the water dropped in little pools all round her. Her choir won.

You imagine the spectators strolling on the grass, the women in sweeping gowns and carrying parasols, bringing their town conventionality to this country place, and enjoying it all immensely. There was the vigour of a new thing about it. One year, as an extra attraction, Blondin, the tight-rope walker, was engaged. He crossed the ravine on a rope, and cooked an omelette in the middle. There is a ring of pride in a dalesman's voice as he tells of this. Blondin was a proof of the importance of the whole affair.

When band contests were started in the Crystal Palace the interest in those at Hardraw waned. The prizes became too small to attract important bands, and eventually the contests ceased. Years later an effort was made to revive them, but the profit for the first year was divided out, leaving nothing in hand for bad seasons, and, as an old lady explaining it said: 'That finished t' lot!'

To stay in Hardraw is to get a feeling of detachment, of having everything which you need close at hand. In two or three minutes you are on the fells, in little more you can be down by the river; and from the west end there is the view up the valley with Appersett sunk under Widdale Fell, and beyond it hill after hill to the head of the dale.

Pen Lane, beside the school at Hardraw, leads up to the fells. Presently it forks, the track on the left going over East Side to Cotterdale. The other, which goes above Hearne Beck, along the side of its desolate ravine, leads to the West Pits, some of the biggest coal pits in the dale. Even at the beginning of this century the roads to the pits were so much used that they looked white instead of green on the fell. About 1911 a rent of three pounds was paid for the West Pits, and about three hundred and ninety tons of coal were dug annually. Now the crumbling walls of its buildings remain as a monument to the days when coal, however poor, was valuable if it was near at hand.

The coal cost two and eightpence for eight hundred-weights, but had to be fetched from the pits, and often this took a whole day. The farmers started in the early morning, when it was dark, and at times the wind was so strong that they thought that they and their carts would be blown over the edge of the track. Sometimes they were lucky and got the coal without much waiting, but often there were so many carts that all they could do was to leave them to be filled, ride their horses home, and return the next day. Some men waited all night to get an early load in the morning. One man started a business of carting coal, charging the same price for it as for the coal. He tells how carts coming from all directions met on the Hardraw road, and how the drivers galloped their horses furiously through the village, trying to get as good a place as possible before they turned up to the moor. The difference in a place might mean an hour's waiting if there was not sufficient coal ready.

These pits have not spoilt the beauty of the moors. The coal was won from levels running into the hill, and but for the tracks and a few ruined buildings you would never know they had been there. It was sold chiefly in the surrounding district where it was used along with peat, and never became a large exporting industry like the lead.

The track to the West Pits is a good route for climbing Shunnor Fell, passing a currack, marked on the map as a beacon, from which there is a magnificent view. A good way down is by the Fossdale Beck. Here dragon-flies skim with their peculiar darting movement over the stream, and rabbits nibble the grass on the banks. It is a softer valley than that of Hearne Beck, merging soon into Clough Wood where there is another waterfall. From here the path goes to the two farmhouses of Fossdale, near which the becks meet on their way to Hardraw.

You come across this corner of Fossdale with surprise, for the cluster of buildings with trees grouped round them have the grace of the valley more than the severity of the moor. It is sometimes thought that it was here —not lower down the valley at Dale Grange, near Askrigg, the recognized site—that Fors Abbey, which was eventually moved to Jervaulx, was founded. The name can be spelt 'Fossdale' or 'Forsdale,' and is always pronounced 'Forzdel' in the district. *Fors* means waterfall, but there is a waterfall near the Askrigg site. Legends have grown round it. People remember being told that a meadow by the beck was said to be a graveyard. Others have heard that across the bridge leading to the last farm was sanctuary. Some years ago a 'jaggle' bell, similar to those which the monks fastened round the necks of their packhorses, was found.

There is an old legend which starts by saying that at the beginning of the reign of Henry VIII the monks of Jervaulx had a small chantry at Hardraw, and the brethren who were in charge of it lived in Fossdale. It tells how Thirler, a hanger-on who lived in the hall at Hardraw,

and Eric, a farmer, had killed a man named Master
Jostrel, who lived near the edge of the scar, and buried
him on the moor. As Jostrel was missing, the monks
decided that he had killed himself, and sent for a brother
from Jervaulx to settle the matter. One stormy night
Eric, to his horror, found the body of Jostrel at the
bottom of Hardraw Scar; they had buried it too near the
beck, and it had been washed out in a flood. This discovery only seemed to confirm the monks' decision, and
they commanded that the body should be buried at the
cross-roads on the moor with a stake through it. One
night, three years later, Eric came to the hall and forced
Thirler to go with him to do penance on Jostrel's grave,
as he himself had done every year. At daybreak a drover
and boy, bringing black cattle across the moor to a fair,
found them clutched together on the grave. Thirler was
dead, his face and right hand burnt, and his knife melted
from the haft. Eric was burnt also, but was still breathing,
and lived long enough to say that they were struggling
with their knives when a thunderbolt struck them. Three
grey stones on the moor are said to mark their graves.

This may be only a tale, but it suggests that there was
some building at Fossdale connected with the abbey,
other than the vaccary for which a subsidy was paid in
1301. Mounds in the meadows by the beck seem to be
foundations of buildings, and mullions of millstone grit
built into the walls and the bridge might have formed
the lights of those buildings. And the peace of the
valley, a stillness which can almost be heard, is like that
which hangs over old ruins. Perhaps the elder tree
which grows where the becks meet, its gnarled and

G

lichen-covered trunk leaning over the water, knows, for it must have been there a long time.

A path from Fossdale joins Pen Lane, going over an enclosure where the grass is coarse and full of rushes, and which in summer is alive with grasshoppers, their metallic chorus ceasing as you approach. The main way out of the valley is through Shaw Gill Wood, crossing the beck by a bridge. When there was only a ford here a man driving a horse and cart from Hawes market was swept down the stream, and he and his horse were only saved from drowning by being caught among the trees. Flagged paths on either side of the beck were made by the Earl of Wharncliffe, who also planted the fir plantations.

At Shaw the road runs into the Buttertubs Pass. This ancient pass between Wensleydale and Swaledale starts half a mile east of Hardraw, and passes the hamlet of Simonstone, where the Earl of Wharncliffe had his shooting lodge, and the name of which means 'Sigemund's rock.' From Shaw it climbs over wild moorland with Shunnor Fell on the west and Stags Fell and Lovely Seat on the east. Just below the summit are the great limestone hollows, the 'Buttertubs,' which give the name to the pass, and beyond them there suddenly appears the romantic valley of Swaledale. The pass is a link between the two dales, whose people, living as they do on either side of one range of hills, have much in common.

The road from the edge of Fossdale is the continuation of Lady Anne Clifford's road from Cotter End. Below Simonstone it turns along the fell to Sedbusk, a mile to the east. In Wensleydale directions are given as east or west, instead of right or left. It is a natural method, for the valley lies in a direct line east and west from Middleham to the Moorcock Inn, but its use has almost a foreign sound.

Sedbusk, a little above the main road, on this side of the valley, is a quaint place which always seems on the point of running away up the fells. Its name means 'the bush near the shieling.' We met an old farmer here who bemoaned the drought. 'We s' all 'ave a famine if it 'ods on,' he said. Drought is a serious thing for these moorland farms, especially in the spring, when grass is wanted to grow for hay in the meadows and feed on the hills. The soil above the rock is so shallow and the fields so brant (steep) that the moisture soon drains away, and the grass, scorched by the sun, has no nutriment.

The farmer told of the days when 'there were so manny sheep on t' mooer, ye could neear tie 'em tail on tail.' 'Why, they're nobbut milk pleeaces noo,' he said. 'When I were a lad we'd pigs an' cauves, an' ducks an' geese, an' butter an' cheese makken. Noo, men weeat gan on to t' farms, they'd rayther wark on t' rooad.'

A lane called Shutt Lane, climbing out of Sedbusk, led to quarries, lead mines, and lime kilns. Many old lime kilns are dotted over the fells and pastures of Wensleydale, generally with good roads leading to them. They are round, built of stone, with a hollow underneath for the fire. Limestone was taken from the fells for burning, and when ready was fetched by the farmers. The kilns are falling into ruin, for when the land is treated now the lime is bought ready for use.

Sedbusk from its ridge on the hill looks across to the town of Hawes. And from Hawes you see it perched there like a half-forgotten outpost.

Bainbridge

CHAPTER VIII

THROUGH BURTERSETT TO BAINBRIDGE

THE main road from Hawes goes down the south side of the valley. Soon a smaller road turns from it to Burtersett, the last of those satellite villages surrounding Hawes. There is a short cut to it by a flagged path across the fields.

The village rests on the hillside, and the summit of Yorburgh, the north end of Wether Fell, rises like a crest above it. Its name means 'the shieling by the alder trees.' It is one of a group of places in this district with names ending in 'sett,' from the Norse word, *sætr*, meaning a shieling, as Appersett and Countersett. In some cases the word 'sett' has been changed into 'side.' There was a very early settlement here, and in the reign of Edward I it had a forest lodge.

Stone quarries were worked extensively behind Burter-

sett in the nineteenth century. An old farmer declares
that it was 'a terrible thrang spot i' them days.' For
many years after the opening of the railway fifteen thousand tons of stone flags were sent from Hawes station
every month. There was a continual trek of wagons,
and to save the road from being cut up two rows of flags
were laid from Hawes to Burtersett. The wagon wheels
rolled on the flags, and the horses walked in the space
between, their feet in wet weather churning it into mud
a foot deep.

Most of the houses built in the district at this period
were of Burtersett stone; the village itself was almost
rebuilt. To-day its tall houses look alien against the
hill, but one or two seventeenth-century houses are left,
of which Hillary Hall is one, and corners of ancient
cottages, and in these the old Burtersett shows. You
get here a sudden feeling of something ancient and remote
which is its real heart, and which outlives changes of
work and ideas.

Old customs survived in Burtersett longer than in
most places. Mell Suppers were kept up after the hay
harvest until well into the present century. At these
there were games and dancing and old songs were sung.
Humour was crude. After one Mell Supper some youths
caught two rams, chained together by their horns as
you often see them in the fields, and just as a farmer
started out for home they let them loose, and sent after
them a dog. The rams' horns knocked together with a
clanging sound, and the terrified farmer hurried along as
fast as he could, sure that a ghost was following him.

The fifth of November was another great day. Piles

of wood and rubbish were collected for the fire for weeks beforehand. The evening started with a procession of young men carrying an effigy of Guy Fawkes, and wearing on their heads blazing barrels which they finally threw on the pile to start the fire. Bonfires are still kept up, and it is typical of dale life that there is one fire for the whole village, not a series of private ones.

The village street, High Lane, continues up the fell, passing a waterfall on Ray Gill, crosses the Roman road, and in a series of twists and curves to avoid the Crag, drops down to Countersett. Another road at the east end of the village leads back to the main road and to Bainbridge.

The entrance to Bainbridge from this side is sudden. You turn a corner between high walls, and the village lies before you. The wide green is crossed by roads, and houses form a ring round it, high on one side and low on the other. They shut in the green from the upper dale and the River Bain, and in their turn are sheltered by the hills of Addlebrough and Wether Fell. Always there is a sense of welcome as you enter, a feeling of having reached a haven, of becoming enveloped in a happy atmosphere. The roads crossing the green leave it so inconspicuously at its four corners that there seems no suggestion of departure.

Houses and shops, chapels and mills, old and new, mingle in a neighbourly manner round the green. The school juts into it, and standing back in a dignified way is the Manor House, rebuilt in its original Tudor style. At the north end, retreating a little from the circle, is the Rose and Crown Inn, with the road from the north side of the valley passing the door. You cannot imagine Bainbridge to-day without its prosperous-looking inn. There was a building here in the fifteenth century, for old writers mention a stone dated 1445 above a round-headed doorway. This, however, has disappeared, and the present carving is a modern copy of old figuring.

At this end, standing in its own burial-ground, is the Quaker meeting-house, built in 1836. It shares with Carperby the distinction of being the only Quaker meeting-houses now used in the dale. The first meetings from 1668 were held in a cottage, now the site of the Temperance Hall, at the opposite corner of the green. It was here that George Fox, the founder of the Quakers, preached.

The oldest part of the village is at the south end, reached by a narrow way called the Newkin. The houses, built at all angles, cluster together, and have a secretive look. Across the mill race a path runs by the River Bain to Semerwater.

The Bain is the shortest river in Yorkshire, being only three miles long. Flowing out of Semerwater, it joins the Ure just below Bainbridge. Camden very aptly describes it as 'a little River comming out of the South called Baint, which with a greate noise streameth out of the Poole Semer.' The whole of its course is steep, and it is a lively river even in dry seasons. Its channel is so deep that it does not often flood, although it rises to the top of the bank, and rushes in a swirling torrent. We watched two ducks unconcernedly nibbling grass on a small island in it, and a duckling swimming in a back-wash at the side, while close by swept a current which would have drowned and beaten to death not only a duck, but a human being. They seemed to have some intuition that the water was not going to rise any more that day, and that they were safe on their island.

The green is the chief glory of Bainbridge to-day. It is the property of the people, who from 1663 have possessed the manorial rights, and a committee called the Lords Trustees of the Manor of Bainbridge still meets. A communal spirit has grown into it. The children play on it, their see-saw presenting a contrast to the ancient stocks, still on their original posts; the boys practise football on it; and in winter its slopes make a fine slide. Cattle and horses graze there. A white horse named Bobby seems a part of it, as permanent as the houses. He takes his share in festivities; in the fancy dress parade on Jubilee Day he gravely drew a wagonette in which sat four Victorian ladies. All the excitements, the fairs, sports, and cricket matches, are held on the green. The old men sit on its seats, smoke their pipes, and talk of the days of their youth.

'Dayleet seeaven,' says one, 'I mortally 'ate it.'

'Aye,' says another, 'what wi' lang neets an' motor bikes an' buses, fooak git ower far afield, an' than they 're neea good for wark i' t' mornin'. When I were a lad, we were nivver called more na' yance. Noo ye can gan up an' shak' 'em tweea-a-three times, an' they weeat git up. Ther 's ower manny pleasures noo-a-days.'

They nod their heads solemnly, then it is all forgotten as they wave a friendly stick to a farmer on his way up the dale. Seeing them you can understand the old man's remark: 'I like a village wi' a green. I could nivver live i' Askrigg.'

One of the loveliest views of the village is from Brough Hill, which encloses it at the west end, and is the site of the Roman fort. Looking east from its summit you see the grace of Wensleydale. It is here that you climb in the early morning after heavy rain for a sight of the flooded valley. It is a fine view-point, easily reached, which is probably why the Romans chose it.

The fort at Bainbridge was excavated by the Yorkshire Archaelogical Society from 1926 to 1931. Traces of a clay-moss rampart and the discovery of certain types of pottery fix the date of the first fort about A.D. 100. Like other Yorkshire outposts, it was destroyed in the great rising of 115, probably by fire, for charred beams, one of which had fallen on to a vase and broken it, were found. It was rebuilt within a few years, this time with a stone wall beyond the rampart of clay, and again reconstructed about 181. The fort was abandoned and probably again destroyed in 275, and rebuilt on a higher level at the beginning of the fourth century. The large number of coins of this period suggest that the last fort was occupied until an unusually late date.

The outer walls were excavated, and four entrances discovered, a chapel, a treasure chamber down some steps, and the commander's and the civilians' quarters. But foundations have to be filled in again, and to the ordinary observer the little things which make the past real are most interesting: the step for mounting chariots, the stone with sockets for the doors. Personal relics are preserved in the museum at Cravenholme Farm just below: fragments of pottery, a small stone altar which a Roman soldier would probably carry on marches, pieces of armour, part of a cheese press, a broken millstone, and a bronze bell. To the farmer's wife at Cravenholme every piece has meaning, many she actually saw excavated. To her the emperors and empresses whose heads are on the coins are people who have lived. 'Now,' she says, as she shows you a coin on which is the head of Marcus Aurelius, 'that's Marcus Aurelius. They do say his wife, Faustina, was the wickedest woman in the world, but Marcus he wouldn't hear a word against her, and when they told me that, I said: "Good old Markie, at any rate there was one man in those days who stuck up for his wife."' Now sheep graze quietly where the Romans lived and used these things which have become museum pieces.

Where the Romans took their legions they made roads. From Bainbridge there was the road over Wether Fell to Ingleton; a road over the Stake Pass to Ilkley; probably one on the north side of the dale to Swaledale and Arkengarthdale; one to Middleham; and there are traces of another at the south-west corner going towards Hawes. Much of these has disappeared, and only the ones over Wether Fell and the Stake Pass have been definitely traced.

But earlier people than the Romans dwelt on Addlebrough, the hill to the south-east of the village. This can be climbed from the lane to Carpley Green, turning near the farmhouse which seems to have hidden away up here from the world. From the summit you seem to see the whole of Wensleydale, up and down. A cairn here may have been the burial-place of Authulf, a British chief from whom the hill gets its name. On both sides of a hollow on the south slope there are remains of hill villages, foundations of small round dwellings, enclosures for sheep and goats, and signs of cultivation of fields. Here where there is now only bent and heather the Iron Age people lived. These upland hollows of Wensleydale are the kind of place they liked, and similar positions were used in other parts of the dale. On the far slope is a burial mound, an immense heap of stones, known as Stone Raise. This has been opened, and a cist found, in which was a skeleton. The origin of the mound is told in a legend which says that a giant passing that way with a heavy chest of gold on his back cried out:

Spite of either God or man,
To Pendragon Castle thou shalt gang,

when the chest fell and sank into the earth, and the stones rose over it. It will be recovered by a mortal to whom a fairy appears as a hen or an ape, but it must be carried away in silence, and without swearing.

Addlebrough can be descended to Thornton Rust, but to return through Carpley Green is to see the hills, which were clear and full of detail when you ascended, blurred and mysterious in the evening light. Then the roofs and chimneys of Bainbridge appear again, and after hours of exploring ancient places the thought of cosy homes and fires becomes very attractive, and your pace quickens as you remember the welcome the village gives.

Perhaps this welcome has come down from the time when Bainbridge was a clearing in the forest, for the

Forest of Wensleydale began here, and extended up the valley to Hell Gill. It was the most important of all the Richmondshire forests. An old manuscript in the possession of the Lords Trustees gives its boundaries: 'The Forest of Wensleydale begins where Bayne water falleth into Yore & so from the water of Bayne up the water of Yore on the far (north) side of the said water to a place called Yore's Head, etc.' Other forest land stretched eastwards from Bainbridge to below Middleham, where the courts for the Richmondshire forests were held, so that the dale was almost uninterrupted forest land, that is wild, uncultivated waste where the lords of the manor hunted deer and stags. At Bainbridge there lived twelve foresters, each of whom had a house, nine acres of grass, and two acres of ploughing land, and two 'grasmani,' the policemen of the forest, whose duty was to arrest evildoers and take them to Richmond Castle, and who also had two acres of land for ploughing between Bainbridge and Golmyrayke, now Goodman Syke.

Dangers surrounded this early village. Wolves and boars roamed the forest, and cattle had to be taken in at night. There were no real roads—by this time the Roman roads had become overgrown—and guides were often employed to show travellers the way. Every evening a horn was blown in Bainbridge to show travellers where they were, a custom which is still kept up. In later years a gun was fired at Camhouse to the north-west, and at Chantry to the east a bell was rung. A toll was charged for going through the forest, but in 1342 only forty shillings was collected, owing, it is said, to the poverty of the travellers. As late as 1609 men remembered the 'guide law,' in which they paid 'thre farthinges to some guyde to gyde them through the forest by reason of the wyldness of the said forrest and for that the same was not inhabyted in former tymes nor passable.'

The forest horn is still blown in Bainbridge. Every night at nine o'clock from 27th September to Shrovetide, three blasts are sounded from the village green. At some time the date has been altered from 14th September, Holy Rood. The horn now used is a buffalo horn, which was presented to the village in 1864 to replace a bullock horn now in Bolton Castle. During the summer it hangs in the hall of the Rose and Crown Inn. Until wireless came, people timed their clocks by it in winter.

The job of blowing the horn is tendered for, but it is generally held for long periods, and often handed down from father to son; many of the hornblowers have been Metcalfes. The present one, who is also the cobbler, has held the post since the war. It is a tying job, but only once has Jamie Metcalfe been more than a few minutes late. That night he went to Askrigg, and was still talking to his friends when he heard the clock strike half-past nine, and realized that the horn should have been blown half an hour earlier. He walked the mile to Bainbridge as quickly as possible, slipped quietly into the house for the horn, sent out three blasts, not too loud that night, and was in the house again before ten o'clock.

'Well,' said his wife when he went into the kitchen, 'what about t' horn?'

'It's late,' he said, 'but I've blown it.'

'They've had a double dose to-night then. Our George blew it at nine o'clock.'

But usually the horn sounds punctually into the night, not very loud if you are inside, but when the wind is in the right quarter it can be heard at Askrigg.

There have been many changes since the forest days, carrying on the progress which began when the Britons first chose their site here. Changes in farming are shown in the field names, not those given on rent rolls, but the names by which the farmers know them. Cravenholme Farm under Brough Hill has these:

High and Low Faudimyin.' (Four days' mowing.)
Corn Close.
High and Low Pluin'. (High and low ploughing.)
Heckberry Hill. (Fruit of bird-cherry tree.)
Lile Hoss Close. (Little Horse Close.)
Stony Hoss Close. (Stony Horse Close.)
Tibby Moor.
Mally. } (Names of people.)
Joney Mecca's Field.

No corn is grown now, and on summer evenings, in haytime, instead of the swish of the scythe there is the rattle of the reaper, taking a few hours instead of four days to mow a meadow. But the village, wrapped in darkness under a dusky sky, must look much the same, and the farmer who bids you good night as he comes through the pastures is a true descendant of those other dalesmen. 'It's a nice quiet night,' he says; 'there's no rain astir.'

CHAPTER IX

RAYDALE AND SEMERWATER

THE road from Bainbridge climbs to Raydale, giving no suggestion of the dale and lake to which it is going. At the top of the first rise the Roman road is seen striking over the fells straight ahead. A green track, outlined with walls, it runs along the lower slopes of the Crag, and climbs Wether Fell, curving near the summit to avoid the highest peak, Drumaldrace, 2,015 feet. A little further on it is joined by the Greensett road, and forks beyond the remote dwellings of Cam Houses at the head of Wharfedale, one way going to Gearstones and the other to Horton-in-Ribblesdale. It has a look of purpose and determination, and is a good example of how the Romans planned their roads to a point on the horizon, and from that to another. In places it has been excavated, and paving found, with a ditch on either side for draining. It was kept in repair when the turnpike road from Richmond to Lancaster was made; later it became a drovers' road; now its chief users are walkers and shepherds.

The Raydale road turns sharply at the junction of the Roman road, and, showing glimpses of the lake, runs past Semerdale Hall to Countersett. This is one of the villages whose name ends in 'sett,' meaning 'shieling'; the first part comes from a proper name, probably 'Constantin,' to whom the settlement would belong. It is a haphazard place. You might fancy the houses were clustered together up the middle when the road came along and swept them on either side; only one cottage dared to creep up again. Each house seems vital to the lay-out, which is one of the great charms of the village. They lie for the most part lower than the road, old houses whose darkened walls have seen happenings which have become history, and sheltered the people who made it. Boar Inn Farm, as its name implies, was once an inn. The date 1667 and a Latin inscription, which means 'Now mine, once thine, but whose afterwards I do not know,' are above the door.

A farmhouse with a large porch is Countersett Hall, remarkable as having been the home of Richard Robinson, the first Quaker in Wensleydale. He was born at Preston-under-Scar in 1628, and, his mother being an heiress, was brought up as a scholar, 'but not at the Universities,' and was inspired to become a Quaker on hearing of the message of George Fox. He was then moved to preach, and travelled over the dales and in many parts of the country—often beaten and imprisoned. Many Quakers visited Countersett Hall, and in 1677 George Fox himself stayed a night here, and is said to have slept in the room over the porch. The interior is still much as he would see it. The stone-flagged kitchen has the old ceiling beams, and in the room beyond is the original oak panelling with cupboards along one wall. The house was referred to locally as Quakers' Hall. Richard Robinson died in 1693, after a meeting held at his house, and was buried in the Friends' burial ground at Bainbridge. It was due to his influence that Quakerism, which flourished all over Wensleydale, was especially strong in Raydale.

Meetings were held in Countersett Hall until a meeting-house was built. This is now let to the Methodists, but it remains as it was when the Friends used it, and they occasionally hold a meeting in it. The cottage standing up on the level of the road has a space behind it where the ponies and donkeys of people coming to meeting were stabled. Later this was a school which most of the older people in the dale attended as children.

There are many instances of persecutions of Quakers in Wensleydale, some of the most zealous persecutors being the Metcalfes of Nappa Hall. They were fined, sometimes hundreds of pounds, for holding meetings; they were put into prison; and their goods were seized because they refused to pay tithes—cheese, wool, and knitted stockings being the most usual articles taken.

The Crag, towering above Countersett and Semerwater, seems to invite you to climb it, and a path starting through a gate on the Burtersett road goes almost to the summit. From here you look down into Raydale, far

H

below. It is summer, and the lake, still and calm, might have dropped from above; cows standing deep in the water make patches of colour amongst the rushes, which line the shores at the head of the lake; a fisherman sits in a boat which sways gently up and down on the water. Stalling Busk rests on the hillside across the lake, with the Stake Pass behind it on its way to Wharfedale. There is a crystallized beauty about this valley of Raydale, a perfection which is slowly revealed. It is in a basin hollowed out of the hills, ending, not in greater barrenness and bleakness, but in wooded hillsides and ravines, in a loveliness which is almost exotic. It was a famous valley for hunting; the name Raydale means 'roebuck valley.' Two small dales run into it: Bardale, bleak and gloomy, and Cragdale, a ravine thick with fir trees.

A steep hill leads from Countersett to the water's edge. The lake, avoided by the villages and houses, has a loneliness which adds to its charm. The waves lap against the side as if they would speak with any one who will listen. It covers a hundred and four acres, but floods to double the size, spreading over the marshy land at the head and the meadows at the foot, and making the road impassable. Uncommon birds haunt the shores, and it is famous for fish. As long as records have been kept it has been let for fishing. At times this was worth forty shillings a year, but in the reign of Edward III it was entered as 'worth nothing because it cannot be let, nor any profit made of it.' The name comes from the Old English *sæ*, sea or lake, and *mere*, which can mean either pool or marsh, giving the whole as meaning a marshy lake.

Semerwater owes its existence to the Ice Age. There was no outlet for the ice from Raydale because of the Wensleydale glacier, in its turn blocked by that of the Vale of York, and as the ice melted drift dammed the foot of the valley, and a large lake was formed, of which this is a remnant. Eventually the water cut a narrow way through the drift, making the course of the River Bain. The Carlow Stone, a large rock shaped at one end like a face, and two stones known as the Mermaid Stones, at the foot of the lake, are all limestone boulders brought down by the ice. There is a tradition that the Carlow Stone was dropped by a giant as he hurled it from Addlebrough at the devil on Crag Hill. The stone which the devil hurled back fell just short of the summit of Addlebrough; it is called the Devil's Stone.

Legend also has another story than that of the Ice Age for the origin of the lake. It says that a beautiful city stood where now it is all water. One day an angel came to the town disguised as a beggar, and knocked at every door begging for bread, but from all he was turned scornfully away. Just outside the city he came to a mean hut in which lived a poor man and his wife. These people invited the stranger in and gave him milk to drink, and cheese and oatcake, and a bed for the night. The next morning he thanked them, and then turned towards the inhospitable city and cried:

> Semerwater rise—Semerwater sink,
> And cover all save this lile house
> That gave me meat and drink.

Immediately there was a terrible noise, the earth sank,

and floods rolled down the hillside, quickly covering the tops of the highest houses. The cottage where the stranger was welcomed was the only one saved, and the man and his wife and their children after them became prosperous. Fishermen have thought they saw the roofs of the city gleaming through the water, and heard the sound of church bells. A ruined cottage at Low Blean on the east side of the dale is pointed out as the one which survived. The late Sir William Watson has told the story in his *Ballad of Semerwater*.

The road from Countersett to the head of the valley runs above the lake on the west side. Beside a beck to the left, and opposite a new cow-house, is a barn which was once a silk mill, though probably worked latterly as a woollen mill. Children used to be sent to the mill every Monday morning with a halfpenny to fetch a bucket of soap-suds which their mothers used for washing clothes. Part of the building was a cottage for the foreman, and continued to be occupied when the mill was closed, chiefly by old men living alone.

One occupant, Humphrey Hopper, used to swim across the lake and back every day, winter and summer. He was notorious for his power of exaggeration; any one telling a particularly unlikely story is still told 'Thou's as big a leear as Aud Humph.' He had a boat in which he used to row visitors on the lake. One day a visitor ridiculed the tale of the buried city under Semerwater, and Aud Humph said he knew it was there because he had seen it. 'I were yance i' this varry booat,' he said, 'fairish out like i' t' middle o' t' laaeke, an' it were a grand loun (calm) day. After a bit I stopped an' started to cut misel a bit o' bacca. I 'd laid mi gully (penknife) down on t' booat edge, an' it tummeled intu t' watter, an' I seed it gan into a square black spot, summat like a shaft. I thowt to misel, 1 'll loup in an' git it out, so I doffed mi cleeas an' dived into t' black hoal. When I gut to t' boddom, I worr in a kitchen an' mi knife were liggin' on t' hearthsteean. So doa't thee tell me thar isn't a city under thar, becos I 've seen it.' 'Aud Humph' always said that when he died he would come back to haunt the district, and he is declared to be seen occasionally riding a white horse.

A house on the left named Carr End was the home of the Fothergill family, who came into Wensleydale in 1606 from Ravenstonedale, and became prominent Quakers. The inscription 'J F 1667' is on a stone over the garden gateway, faintly incised on the outside and carved in relief on the inside. John Fothergill of Carr End made three journeys to America, the first in 1721. His son, John Fothergill, born here in 1712, became a noted doctor in London, and in 1779 founded Ackworth School, the northern Friends' school for boys and girls. Another son, Samuel, was a great Quaker preacher. Alexander, a younger son, was a road surveyor, and one of the most influential men in Wensleydale in the late eighteenth century. He left a diary which unfortunately cannot now be traced. Miss Jessie Fothergill, a popular novelist at the end of the nineteenth century, was a descendant of his, and Wensleydale is the scene of her book, *Kith and Kin*. Carr End passed out of the hands of the Fothergills in 1842.

It is an experience to take the road up Raydale when

haymaking is in full swing. This is no ordinary time in the dales. It is talked of and planned for weeks beforehand; now rain is wanted for the grass, now sun, and for long afterwards its goodness or its badness is discussed. In a district where there is only one harvest, that one is vital. All the family are needed in the hay-fields. The Yorebridge Grammar School falls in with it, and breaks up early for the summer holidays or half its children would be missing. The outside helpers are chiefly Irishmen who come to the dales after they have helped with the hay in lower districts, but sometimes a boy or girl is hired as a haytime leader to ride the horses.

The work is concentrated, often the workers belonging to one farm are all in one field. Here where the weather is uncertain the farmer cuts only a small quantity of grass at once, and aims to get it in as quickly as possible. The processes follow each other with little break from the first strewing to the loading on to carts or sledges. Sledges are used more than carts because the hay, being stored in barns, not in a central stackyard, has often to be taken no further than the next field. On the hillier ground it is gathered up by a wooden contrivance called a 'tip catch,' pulled by a horse.

Walter White during his journey through Yorkshire in 1858 helped to make hay in Raydale, and says in his book, *A Month in Yorkshire*, that 'haymaking with the blithesome lassies in Ulrichsthal is a much more sprightly pastime than haymaking with the Quakers in Wensleydale.' He would find the haymakers gay enough to look at nowadays in their bright dresses and white hats, but he would find the same seriousness. Strangers to whom at other times the people would be glad to talk are unnoticed. It is a world of hay.

The road comes into the village of Marsett, which, even in normal times, is an unusual place to find. A stone bridge over the beck leads to a stretch of common land, bordered on one side by the beck and on the other by the few houses. It has a medieval air. You can imagine news of a raid reaching the village, and cattle and sheep being brought down from the hills to this enclosure where they could be watched. One of the fields has the name 'Knight's Close,' and is the site of an old hall.

Ordinarily the village seems asleep, as if time had stood still in this remote corner, shut in by hills, and on the road to nowhere. But in haytime it is like a picture of old English country life. A group of women move out from a farmhouse; a girl sits bare-backed on a horse, driving a load across the common; at a barn a man tips off her load and turns the horse back, before tossing the hay through an opening in the upper story, into which an invisible hand drags it; a tiny child plays naked about the beck. Two gipsies with a donkey cart have pulled up on the common, and loll lazily under the wall. Then the woman rises, stretches herself, and fetches the materials for a fire. When it burns she places a pan on it, and brings from the cart bread and cheese for a meal, moving with a slow, lithe grace. The feverish activity around contrasts with their air of leisure, their taking of each day as it comes with little thought for the future. Theirs is the freedom, but not the satisfaction of the newly-filled barns.

A road runs out of Marsett to Raydale Grange, and, a mile beyond it, to Raydale House, which has a fine position looking down the valley. The house was largely rebuilt in the nineteenth century, but parts of the seventeenth-century building are left. In 1617 it was besieged by Sir Thomas Metcalfe, the 'Black Knight of Nappa.' The estate of Raydale had been let to him in 1609–10 by the king, but he mortgaged it to William Robinson of Worton for a thousand pounds. He was to pay a hundred pounds a year, and have the option of buying it back after six years. At the end of seven years he had paid nothing, and William Robinson took formal possession, and placed his son as tenant there. Sir Thomas, angry at having lost it, laid siege to the house. The siege lasted four days, but help was obtained from York, and Sir Thomas was defeated, one of his men being killed.

The road stops at the house, but a path leads across Cragdale to Stalling Busk on the east side of the valley. Longdale House, now a ruin, near the top of Cragdale, is said to have been the first house in Raydale. An old woman who lived here used to walk the three miles to Stalling Busk church and back every Sunday when she was over ninety. Her ruined house with trees protecting it has still a homely air, although it must have been one of the loneliest houses in Wensleydale. Sheep from lower farms are grazed on the moors above Cragdale, and an old farmer tells how his flock, sensing a coming snowstorm, came 'tip-top fra' Cregdel like yan man,' and saved him the trouble of fetching them.

From Marsett to Stalling Busk there is only a cart-track, but the two villages are very much connected.

The church and schools for both are at Stalling Busk. Unlike Marsett, this village perches on the hillside, and has a view of the lake and of Bardale. Here again there are ruined houses, and the village has an anxious look, as if it wonders how long it will last. There seems no centre; ways cross at various angles, and before you feel to have arrived you are at the other side. There is now a modern church in the village. The older church is in ruins at the foot of a hill near the lake, but its church-yard is still the graveyard for the dale.

The people had a struggle to get this first church, to keep it, and to find suitable ministers for it. It was built in 1603 on a piece of common land at the cost of the inhabitants. During the Civil War it fell into ruin, but on fine Sundays services were held in it, and on wet Sundays in a house. In 1722, the common land being then enclosed, the inhabitants bought the old chapel garth, rebuilt the church, and appointed a curate, Anthony Clapham, with a stipend of twenty-seven pounds, five shillings. But their affairs did not go smoothly, and the Bishop of Chester, to whose diocese Stalling Busk belonged, was besieged with letters from them asking him for help. There were differences with Aysgarth as to whether baptisms, marriages, or funerals should be held at the church instead of at Askrigg; disputes over choosing their own curates; trouble with curates who made agreements without their knowledge; and dissatisfaction with curates who did not reside in the parish. One of these employed a man to take the services, giving him ten pounds a year, a sum on which the man, who had a wife and three children, found it hard to live. The old letters, still preserved, tell the story, and how the bishop, far away in another county, was not for long allowed to forget this tiny chapel on the fells of Raydale.

The old chapel looks peaceful now. It was a peculiar building with nave and aisles running from north to south. The altar was in the middle of the long east aisle, and the pews were arranged transversely to the arcade to face it. The interior fittings have gone, and there is no roof, but the people still have a possessive feeling about the church, and carefully tend the ivy which climbs the piers.

The lane out of Stalling Busk meets the Stake Pass road from Wharfedale just above the village. Presently it passes High Blean Farm, which is said to have been given to General Lambert for bravery at the Battle of Waterloo. Now it crosses a beck on which there are two waterfalls, High and Low Force. For a time, looking back, there are beautiful views of the lake, then the road drops suddenly on its way down to Bainbridge, and the hill shuts off the lake and the valley, hiding them from all but those who go to seek them.

Coleby Hall

CHAPTER X

BAINBRIDGE TO ASKRIGG

BAINBRIDGE and Askrigg, though so different, form the strongest of the pairs of villages characteristic of Wensleydale. In the mile between them lies much of the history of the dale. Hamlets are grouped along it, each with connections in the two villages, and helping to draw them together. The River Ure divides them, and is crossed by a bridge named Yore Bridge, built at the end of the eighteenth century to replace an earlier one.

A building just before the bridge is the old Yorebridge grammar school, with the head master's house close to it. The school was founded in 1601 when Anthony Besson, having found a need for better education in the district, gave two houses in Coney Street, York, to maintain a master to teach 'the children of the chapelry.' The school was free except for a 'cockpenny,' paid at Shrovetide, sixpence, a shilling, or two and sixpence, as the parents could afford. In 1879 the boys were paying five shillings a quarter, except for six or eight boys, who got wood and water for the head master.

At times the people were careless of their advantages in having the school. A letter to the *Wensleydale Advertiser* in 1845 says that it had two hundred pounds endowment, and no pupil. Perhaps the letter did good, for in 1848 the school was enlarged. It remained a grammar school, but the work was slack. The master was fond of fishing, and not anxious to give much time to the boys, contenting himself with neglecting them and then punishing them to make up for it. After 1867 the school gradually became a force in the dale. There are old and young men who received their education here whose lives, even if they have never done more than become small farmers and shepherds, show its influence in their minds and outlook. Others have made a name in the bigger world. Girls were admitted in 1919.

In 1931 a new school was built nearer to Askrigg. Children make long journeys to it, you see them in their gay caps and blazers in villages miles away; it has been calculated that the average distance travelled daily by each scholar is seven miles. Wensleydale is fortunate to have retained its grammar school so far up the dale. It has not, like many such schools, become merged in the National School, nor has it become a famous public school like Sedbergh or Giggleswick. The dale gets the best advantage from it as it is. The old school is now used for woodwork classes.

Another influence in this part of the dale has come through the classes started by Mr. T. W. Grubb in 1911.

These took various subjects, but chiefly literature, out of which there grew a dramatic society eager to produce good plays. These classes have given to the members a knowledge and love of literature above the average, and as a result many have taken up careers which otherwise they would never have considered.

The River Bain joins the Ure just below the grammar school, and beyond the meeting there is a natural swimming-pool. From Yore Bridge a flagged footpath runs through the fields to Chantry Farm, crossing Grange Beck. The farmhouse stands on historic ground, the more recognized site than that at Fossdale of Fors Abbey, the first abbey in Wensleydale. Here for eleven years in the reign of Stephen a little group of monks strove against the bleak climate, rough land, and dangers of the forest. They were led by Peter de Quincy, a monk from the abbey of Savigny in Brittany, who had frequented the court of Earl Conan at Richmond. They were anxious to form a Cistercian abbey, and Akar Fitz Bardolph, a relation of the earl's, gave them land at Worton and Fors. When the foundations were laid the earl came with several knights and said: 'Now are we all mighty men, and men of great possessions; let us, therefore, stoutly lay to our hands, and aid it with lands and rents.' More land was given in Burton and Abbotside, and the right of mowing grass in the forest, felling timber for buildings, and working lead and iron: also the monks were allowed to take the remains of deer killed and partly devoured by wolves.

In 1145 the foundation of the oratory was laid. But the Abbot of Savigny was angry with Peter de Quincy for settling in so wild and remote a place, and after five years he refused the government of the new monastery. Peter pleaded with him. 'Blessed be God!' he said, 'within a few years from our first establishment we have now five carucates under the plough; forty cows with their followers; sixteen mares with their foals, the gift of Earl Conan; five sows with their litters; three hundred sheep; about thirty hides in the tannery; wax and oil which will supply our light for two years; and I am very certain that we shall be able to raise a competent supply of ale, cheese, bread, and butter, and that we shall be able to sustain a regular convent out of such beginnings until it shall please God to provide better for them.'

His pleading failed, and the monastery was placed under the government of Byland. An abbot was elected from Byland, and it was then that the name 'Fors' seems to have been dropped, for he was elected with the words: 'Thou art Abbot of Joreval.' Lauric, the cellarer, was commanded to carry the best bell from the old parish church at Byland to Fors, and the colony of abbot and nine monks set out with the rule of order and box of relics for Fors. The first night they rested in a village, and here the abbot had a dream. He was at Byland, and saw a beautiful woman walking in the cloister, holding by the hand a boy whose countenance was as the moon for brightness. The boy plucked a branch from a tree in the cloister, and vanished. Then in the abbot's dream he and the monks were on their journey again, and had lost their way amongst the rocks and bushes. They said their hours and gospel, and the woman and the child appeared again.

'Fair and tender woman,' the abbot cried, 'what doest thou with thy son in this rugged and desert place?'

'I am a frequent inmate of desert places,' she answered, 'but now I have come from Rivaulx and Biland, with whose abbots I am familiarly acquainted, and am going to the new monastery.'

'Good lady, I implore thee to conduct me and my brethren out of this desert place, and lead us to the new monastery, for we are of Biland.'

'Ye were late of Biland, but now of Jorevale.' Then, turning to the boy, she said: 'Sweet son, be their leader, I am called elsewhere,' and vanished.

The boy cried, 'Follow me,' and led them, still holding in his hand the bough he had picked at Byland, till he came to a barren place. Here he planted the bough, which had become full of white singing-birds, and said: 'Here shall God be adored for a short space.' So the abbot knew by his dream that they were not to stay long at Fors.

Before daybreak they moved on. Dogs barked as they passed, and at dawn the people peeped out at them and said: 'These are the abbot and monks passing from Biland to Jorevale.' One old man looked at the stars and said: 'They have chosen a fortunate time, for within thirty or forty years they shall attain a state of worldly glory, from which they shall never fall.'

The abbey did not prosper as Peter had hoped. There were bad seasons for crops, they were troubled by wolves, and probably plundered by the people. After four disastrous years there was a fifth even worse, and

five of the monks were sent back to Byland and three to
Furness. Two years later Earl Conan, returning from
France, saw their plight, and gave them another pasture
in Wensleydale and presently a tract of land below
East Witton, to which the house was transferred, and
grew into the abbey of Jervaulx. The monk, Peter, he
took back to his court.

Remains of Fors Abbey can be seen in a trefoiled
window at the back of the farmhouse, and a flat-headed
doorway. The railway line cut through the burial-
ground, and during its building many human bones were
found. A grange and a chantry chapel were kept up
here as long as Jervaulx Abbey was occupied. When
Fors was dismantled at the Dissolution it had one bell.

The eleven years which the monks spent at Fors were
years of hard work and much suffering and disillusion-
ment. The sadness of their failure, the slow hopelessness,
seems to linger over this area. The train runs above it,
and in summer the shouts of bathers in the pool in the
river are heard, but they cannot destroy the remembrance
of a hope which had to be abandoned. This is rich
pasture and meadow land now, but it is too exposed and
open to all weathers to have supplied in those days the
needs of a growing community of men. It has not the
graciousness of most abbey sites. But you admire the
little group who stood it so long. In the gentler house
at Jervaulx, and the court at Richmond, they must have
thought sometimes with longing of their first venture.
Perhaps our modern love for hills and moors was in them
too, making them willing to settle so far up the dale.
The house at Chantry is haunted, not as you might hope

by one of the monks, but by a little man dressed in green who is seen passing round the back of the house.

The hamlet of Bowbridge to the west has lost some of its character by the widening and altering of the road. This formerly curved backwards over a bridge which tradition ascribes to the monks of Fors, and which has been preserved. It was widened in the eighteenth century when Alexander Fothergill was surveyor of the roads. Many of the road improvements of this district and the bridges of the period are due to his influence.

Roads in the early seventeenth century were bad around Askrigg, and John Coleby, who had a house at Bowbridge, where the Methodist chapel now stands, is said to have had a winter residence in Askrigg, opposite the King's Arms Hotel. In 1655, having purchased a third of the manor and forest of Abbotside, John Coleby built Coleby Hall on the hill behind Bowbridge, using for it a doorway and many of the stones from the ruins of Fors Abbey. A curse was supposed to fall on him because of this, for he was thrown from his horse and killed on the road from Bainbridge just after the house was completed.

A family named Scarr then came to Coleby Hall as tenant-farmers, and their descendants have occupied it to the present day. At first there was only one large pasture, and they set to work to reclaim the moor, enclosing piece after piece and liming and draining it. Succeeding generations took up the work, until it became one of the finest farms in the district. In 1932 Mr. James Scarr bought the Hall.

Some of its oak chests and pewter plates and dishes are nearly as old as the walls, and inside and out there is

I

about this manor house a feeling of peace and security which defies the change and restlessness of to-day.

A lane from Bowbridge climbs the steep hillside, and soon meets the continuation of Lady Ann Clifford's road, which has run down the valley parallel with the present road but higher up the fell. It has come from Sedbusk through the hamlets of Litherskew and Shaw Cote. In the fields below these, between the old and the new roads, is the site of the hamlet of Holehouse, mentioned in seventeenth-century records as having three farmhouses. It is now one of the lost villages of Wensleydale — the foundations of two houses can be traced in the grass, and against the wall is an aged plum tree.

From Shaw Cote the road turns up the fell, to drop down to the hamlet of Skellgill. On it we found a small boy and a dog watching a man drive poles at intervals along the top of the wall and fasten wire to them. The wall looked high, but it was not high enough to keep out the sheep. As the farmer explained: 'It seems as if it's born in 'em, is jumpin'.' Perhaps because their principal use is to prevent sheep from straying, the dalespeople do not call these boundaries 'walls,' but 'fences.'

Skellgill is said to have been an important place with three inns in the packhorse days. Now it consists of four farmhouses. You come across it with surprise, for, lying in a hollow, shut in on all sides, it is not visible from the valley. When this was the main road, Skellgill would be a sheltered haven for travellers to reach. Now it has a forgotten air, a loneliness which has more sadness in it than the loneliness of the moors. An arched bridge crosses the stream, but little traffic goes over it. The first time we went to Skellgill we found a row of dead rats nailed by their tails to the branch of a tree by the stream. Their sleek corpses hanging there in shame had a sinister look.

A track goes up the fell behind Skellgill to the Sargill lead mines, the oldest and some of the richest in Wensleydale. They were owned for some time by two brothers, a solicitor and a parson, named Winn, who to save carrying the lead to the smelt mills over the hills in Swaledale, built a smelt mill here, the ruins of which and those of the changing-house remain. At one time the lead appeared to be failing, and they accepted the offer of a Swaledale miner to take the mine and look for lead. After much bargaining they agreed that if the Swaledale man found lead he should give the brothers so much a bing, but that if he found no lead he should pay nothing.

'Well,' said the parson owner, 'ye can go and wark now then.'

'Nay, I mun have a bargain on paper. Ah doa't mistrust ye av coorse, but it 's nobbut biznuss.'

The agreement being made and signed, he set to work. He dammed the stream and 'hushed' the hill, found great quantities of lead, and made a fortune. The brothers were furious, but all the miner said was: 'It 's minin' proper.'

From Skellgill the road is a narrow, walled lane, with a scattered farmhouse here and there along it. Luke's House must have received its name in the early seventeenth century, for it is given in the Abbotside Survey of about 1603 as 'the Widdow of Luke Thwaite house, but newly built, with barn, stable, turfhouse, and garden.' This road, except for the surface, gives an idea of what the dale roads were like in packhorse days, when they were known as 'jagging roads.' It is narrow and winding, now open, now enclosed, going with a leisurely yet a businesslike air, an essential part of the scene, yet never intruding. Running as it does along the hills, some of the finest views are to be had from it, showing the dale from a new angle. The view from near Spen House is magnificent in its scope and variety. The packmen and drovers must have gone slowly and blithely along this piece, making the most of their chance of company at the groups of houses before they turned on to the lonely fells.

Turning to the right above Coleby, the road runs to Helm, generally pronounced 'Hellum,' another hamlet whose importance went when the road ceased to be a highway. There are now only two farmhouses and a few derelict ones. In the garden of one of these a plum tree blooms, as if it did not know that the house for which it was planted is deserted.

The track crosses Whitfield Beck at Slape Wath, a little above Mill Gill Force, a beautiful waterfall reached over a rustling carpet of beech nuts. A mile higher up the beck is Whitfield Force, a lovely but quite different fall. These are two of the finest falls in the dale. At the next farm, New Park, the right of way goes through an outbuilding which has been made over a public footpath.

Lady Ann Clifford's road runs along the fell, coming

out into the Muker road above Askrigg.   In her journey
to Nappa Hall Lady Ann would keep along the slope of
Nappa Scar, and come down through Nappa village to
the present road, but a continuation of the road from
Westmorland goes over Windgates to Whitaside in
Swaledale, and so to Barnard Castle.   Windgates means
'wagon road.' This, the first road up the dale, was a
track in very early times, connecting places beyond, as
do the modern Wensleydale roads.

Askrigg Old Hall

CHAPTER XI

ASKRIGG

ASKRIGG seen from a distance is one of the pictures in Wensleydale which never lose their freshness. From each side it is different. Seen from the south it rests under Ellerkin; from the east it seems flung into the valley, dwarfed by the hills beyond; from the Swaledale road its roofs and steep street have a soft appearance, very different from the west approach where it grimly climbs the hillside with the church at the end guarding it. Seeing it in winter across the snow-covered valley, the walls of the houses show dark against the surrounding whiteness, like children in cosy caps, and only the cottage lights twinkling in the frosty air tell of its reality. From far and near there is enchantment in the view, so that you enter Askrigg with anticipation. And you are not disappointed.

Turning past the first houses the road runs into a cobbled market-place with a market cross, on one side the church, and on another the ruins of a Caroline manor house. Then the street narrows, and tall houses line it on both sides, until suddenly there are cottages again, and the village is left behind by a road which goes down the valley and another which climbs the moor. Askrigg should be taken first in a swinging stride, seeing its beauty as a whole; there will be time later to explore it.

The first village started at the east end near the beck. There is a field here known as Kirk Close, where a Saxon church or a preaching cross may have stood. After the present church was built in the thirteenth century at the west end, Askrigg grew in this direction, but it grew not as a village, but a town. Besides the farms and the mills, industries and crafts were developed, lead mining, knitting, and clockmaking; and it was the market town for the upper dale. The market has gone, and the old industries, though some new ones have taken their place. But its past importance clings to its church and to the tall houses with their curiously detached air. They are town houses. As you walk up the street you feel your ignorance of all that goes on behind those walls; there is a feeling which houses in quiet London streets give of people in them who do not know you, and of whom you know nothing. Its people are townspeople, they have no doubt that Askrigg is the centre of the dale, that it leads and other places follow; and unconsciously they have taken on some of its dignity.

But if Askrigg has the atmosphere of a town, it has none of a town's disadvantages. Fells roll back from it, and meadows creep up to it. This is the quieter side of the valley; and the people still walk on the road instead of the pavement, and they dislike crowds.

No church in the dale has a finer position than Askrigg church, looking eastward over the square and the life of the village, and westward over Yorebridge School to the hills. Its tower, yellowed with age, seems to exult in the storms they can bring. In the churchyard are the tombs of the dalespeople; on some their occupation, such as hosier or clockmaker, is given; and it is proud of its tombstone of 'an honest attorney' who died in 1746.

A church was built about 1100, the tower added in the fifteenth and the aisles and clerestory in the early sixteenth century. The roof is covered with lead from local mines, and when recast in 1824 was found to weigh 995 stone. The massive circular columns of the north arcade are sometimes thought to have come from Fors Abbey, but it is unlikely that Fors in its short life had masonry so imposing.

The south or Metcalfe chapel was founded in 1468 by James Metcalfe of Nappa Hall, and the last of his direct descendants was buried there in 1756. The old parish chest remains, and the painted clock over the south door with an inscription whose punctuation adds to its charm: 'Deface; me not. I mean no; ill I. stand, to serve; You for good will.' The silver chalice is dated 1666. Some of the carved bench-ends of the old pews are still preserved in the village, and the brass plates engraved by one of the clockmakers with the names of the owners.

A pew in the church was often included in the sale of property.

On Sunday evenings the lighted windows of the church send their glow into the square, as they have done for centuries of Sundays; through one can be seen the slow, regular movements of the organ blower. He seems to stand for all those who in the past have taken their part in the life of the village, and to link them up with those who to-day are moulding it for the future.

There is a notice in the church registers of the baptism of 'a foundling left at Askrigg upon the hard stones, by a woman unknown, on St. Luke's Day, 1780.' With that happy knack of choosing appropriate names, characteristic of the dale, the child was called Luke Stones.

In October 1935, Askrigg Old Hall, one of the treasures of Wensleydale, was destroyed by fire. Its dignified walls were so much a part of the market square and of all Askrigg, that its destruction is felt like the loss of a friend. This Caroline manor house was built in 1678 by William Thornton. A stone over the door records this, and has a text from Hebrews in Latin: 'For every house is builded by some man; but he that built all things is God.' The oak beams and panelling and the studded doors perished, but the wooden gallery which runs over the doorway was not touched. It is said to have been erected for the inhabitants to watch the bull-baiting, the stone and ring for which are still on the cobbles below. It used to be a custom in Askrigg for a man who wanted to fight to go and turn the bull ring over; if another man was feeling the same, he came and turned it back, and they had a fight.

The King's Arms Hotel and two houses next to it were built by John Pratt, Esq., as one private house. It was sold in the nineteenth century, and the buyer received as much for the massive lead pipes as he had paid for the house; there is one left with the date 1767 on it. The King's Arms Hotel has several oak chests and a beautiful refectory table which belonged to the house. John Pratt, who died in 1785, made money as a jockey at Newmarket, and became a breeder of racehorses, one of which he sold to the Prince of Wales. He kept a pack of hounds, the kennels for which are built round a sunken circle at the back of the house. In the stables behind, at the top of the stairs leading to the lofts, a trap-door covers a fox hole where captured foxes were kept for hunting.

Askrigg's market charter, which also allowed two annual fairs, was granted to Peter Thorneton by Queen Elizabeth, 'to lighten the grievous journeys and labours which the inhabitants of that town would be compelled to go by resort to other markets very remote,' and to repay the industry of those who had formed it. There were fears of losing the market trade as early as 1725, for in that year the profits of the tolls were used for a lawsuit to prevent Hawes from having a market. It failed, and slowly the business went from Askrigg there.

Under the market charter a body of four men was elected annually by the people to regulate the tolls, and have the custody of the toll-booth. At first a custom prevailed called the 'house row,' by which the profits of the tolls were distributed from house to house. Later they were used chiefly for the improvement of the market-place, and prizes were given at the fairs.

Some of the account books of the 'Four Men' are preserved. There are many entries for dressing and cleaning the market-place. This would be very necessary, for dirt and refuse was dumped there, especially round the cross. In 1731 3s. 4d. was given to Edward Metcalfe for '5 days shouling & filling the cart.' In that year a tree was bought for 12s. to make stalls, 1s. 6d. was paid for felling and leading it, and 7s. for working it. The market-place was paved in 1735; the market cross was restored in 1746, and the present one built in 1851. Sometimes unexpected money was received, as when some 'players acting one night' paid 6d. There are less prosaic entries, as in 1746 when 10s. was given 'to rejoicings of the victory over the rebells.' It seems that Askrigg did not favour the Young Pretender.

As prizes at the fairs they paid £1 10s. in 1731 for a 'saddle, bridle & hatt to be run for,' and in 1739, 5s. 'for asses to run for.' In 1758 there was given 'To George Tular for traill & cat, 1s. 3d.'; evidently a cat was killed and its body trailed for the dogs to scent. In 1751 6s. was paid 'to George Fowler & John Metcalfe for attending with halberts during the fair.' Perhaps in 1822 one or all of them had been caught by awkward questions, for in that year they gave a guinea to 'Mr. Fidler for translating the charter.' In 1895 the 'Four Men' came to an end, their duties being taken over by the Parish Council, who in 1898 sold the toll-booth, which was later pulled down. This custom of ruling themselves developed independence and self-reliance.

The 'Four Men' were chosen from the people; rich and poor stood the same chance.

Clockmaking was one of the most important industries. During part of the eighteenth century there were more clocks made in Askrigg than anywhere else in the North Riding. Clockmakers first appeared in Wensleydale in the seventeenth century. The oldest known was James Ogden of Bowbridge, who was in business before 1690. The first Askrigg makers were Mark Metcalfe; James Wilson, who died in 1780; and Christopher Caygill, who died in 1803. Their clocks had only one hand, and they introduced arched faces, generally of brass. Men were apprenticed to the trade, and some of these, like Thompson and Sagar, having learnt their craft, went to other parts of the country. Often an apprentice married one of the master's daughters—a John Stansfield married Caygill's daughter. He was an apprentice along with James Pratt, into whose family the Askrigg business passed, going from father to son, and finally to a nephew, John Skidmore, whose son still has the shop. The Pratts made only painted faces.

Mr. Skidmore has the tools which his father and the older clockmakers used; they are hand-made, many of them fine and delicate. Every part of the clock was made by hand, and the tools were invented as they were found necessary. The anvil is the trunk of a tree about two and a half feet high, with a block of iron on the top, and is called a 'stiddy.' The bow drill, made of a hazel twig, string, a wooden spindle, and a drill, would bore through wood or metal. There are three sizes of bows; in the smallest horsehair was used instead of string.

Another small tool, called the 'mouse's claw,' was twirled on the end of a rod to round off edges. There are also engraving tools for putting names on the clocks. Little change was made in the works, though Pratt introduced a few small improvements. One of the first jobs an apprentice was set to do was to make the chain for the pendulum. One of the most skilful jobs was to hammer a piece of metal perfectly flat. The clockmaker did not as a rule make the case, but employed the same casemaker. All was very orderly in the clockmaker's shop, but it was a social place, especially for the men of the village, who would sit round the fire watching the work and telling tales for hours.

There was excitement over the packing and delivery of the finished clock, which required two men to carry it. It was laid across their shoulders, the movement resting in a butter basket which one of them carried on his arm, and thus it was taken, always by hand, often many miles, to its first home. Many of the Askrigg clocks went to Swaledale. A thirty-hour clock cost about three pounds a hundred years ago, and an eight-day clock five pounds. A grandfather's clock was one of the first pieces of furniture a couple about to be married would come and order; without one they would not have felt themselves properly married. The introduction of American clocks killed the industry.

There were three mills to the west of Askrigg, all built along the same beck, and using its water for their power. The lower one was a woollen mill, the middle a flax mill, which seems to indicate that flax was once grown in the dale, and the top one, West Mill, was a corn mill.

A walled lane above the church goes to West Mill.

Approaching it you get a sensation that if you breathe heavily the whole will collapse. The roof overhangs, and you bend instinctively to go under it, although it is quite high. At the side is the water wheel which, unless the weather is very dry, still works the mill; but it turns now, not to grind corn, but to saw wood. Hayrakes are made here. Rakes, or parts of them, are everywhere: finished ones stacked in outbuildings ready for packing, piles of long handles waiting to be attached, hundreds of curved pieces wedged between beams to keep them from going straight again—they have been bent after being soaked in water. Narrow outside steps climb into the mill, and here there is the sound of the saw and the smell of newly cut wood, pine for the handles and ash for the rest. A machine invented by the miller's father stamps out the wooden teeth, but the rakes are assembled by hand.

This has been a corn-grinding mill in the life of the owner. When corn was no longer grown in the district it was bought in the markets, ground here, and delivered in the district. The men who delivered it, first on packhorses and then with carts, were known as 'badgers,' and these men were a familiar sight in the dale. Formerly the farmers of Upper Swaledale had their corn sent from the markets to Askrigg, where it was stored in the mill and ground as they wanted it, and every few weeks they would come over the moor with a horse and cart and take back a load. Road transport changed that, nor could these small mills fight against the bigger ones with capital behind them to buy new machinery as it came along, and scrap it as some better invention quickly followed.

The beck which drives the water wheel also works the

electric plant which lights Askrigg, the power coming chiefly from the waterfall. It was the first village in the dale, and one of the first in England to be lit by electricity. Askrigg is also one of the places which have a dairy. When this was first started by Mr. Richard Mason, milk from his own and one more farm was made into cheese. Now as many as a thousand gallons are taken in a day.

A pasture up the Swaledale road is known as the Garland Field, because a lady who had had a disappointing love affair left it in her will, the rent to be used to provide an annual prize for which the young men of Askrigg were to run a race. It was a stiff race over the fells, and at the end the winner was given a garland to wear.

Higher still, on a road to the right, is a flat enclosure on the slope of Ellerkin, known as the Fair Allotment. Here an annual horse fair was held, and became famous as Askrigg Hill Fair. It began in 1785, further down the dale, in a field called Carperby Sleets, with a few lots of sheep which were unsold at Stagshaw Bank Fair in Northumberland. After fourteen years it was moved to Askrigg Moor, then unenclosed. When the Enclosure Act was passed in 1817 it was held for two or three years at Gaudy, near Gayle. Askrigg Moor was enclosed 1819–20, and as the site was not spoilt the fair was again held there. It was primarily a horse fair; there were galloways bred on the surrounding moors; hundreds of horses brought by gipsies who raced them on the allotment; and great numbers of sheep, cattle, goats, and pigs were penned on the moor. There were also booths and shows, and gipsies telling fortunes. It was a general holiday, and people came long distances to it.

An old lady lower down the dale remembers as a child helping to dig peats on the moor, and being told that as a reward she should be taken to Askrigg Hill Fair. A Mr. Law, a schoolmaster of Hawes and Thoralby, used to make his scholars compose verses on the fair. Here is one written in 1847:

> Stallions proud with ribbands prancing,
> Joyous fiddling and dancing.
>
> Isaac Horsfield who was there,
> He made sport for all the fair.
>
> A handsome show of china ware,
> Of much variety was there.
>
> Cheese-cakes plenty might be got,
> Ginger bread and good tom-trot.

The glory of the fair, like that of many more, went with the coming of motors, but an annual horse fair, still known as Askrigg Hill Fair, is held in the market-place. The chief sellers now are the gipsies, and their customers mostly farmers who need an extra horse for haytime. There are only between thirty and forty horses altogether, but something of the spirit of the old fair lingers. The men lounge on the cobble stones, leaning against the churchyard wall, yet alert for buyers. Before them are rows of horses, tied together, but loosened in an instant if there is the chance of a customer. Little boys, horse dealers of the future, sit patiently on carts, drinking lemonade from bottles. The horses are run and galloped up and down the steep main road, their owners dragging at the cart wheels to show how well they pull, and climbing about their hind legs to prove that nothing will make them kick. The old way of carrying on and concluding a bargain is retained. The seller holds out his hand, which the bidder strikes as he makes an offer. If the seller hits back with two fingers he means that they are still good friends, but he could not take such a ridiculous bid. So they go on until their prices come nearer together, and an offer is finally accepted, when the seller strikes the buyer's hand with his own. After the farmers have bought, the gipsies bargain amongst themselves.

At one time there was great rivalry between Wensleydale and Swaledale men, and Askrigg Hill Fair generally ended in fights between them. In 1935 the most friendly sale of all was to a Swaledale man. Every one came to look at his purchase during the afternoon, and as he rode away on his sturdy little horse, the Askrigg men called out: 'Aye, it's a gran' lile hoss ye 've gitten.'

Whilst the men are bargaining, the potter women are going from door to door selling their pots and brushes. Presently they will drive away, many in cars, but a few still go with their horses to camps on the green roads near the old allotment, where groups of children watch anxiously for them. There will be a meal round a table in the open air, then a quick packing before they move along the narrow road to their next place of call.

Some of the Scotch dealers who sent cattle to the fairs were wealthy men. It was common knowledge that they carried large sums of money about with them, and there were many instances of violent deaths on the moors. From one of these murders comes the tale of the Scotch lord in Askrigg. His name seems to have come

K

from the Scotch 'laird,' but why he should have been called this no one knows. The tragedy happened over a hundred years ago. The Scotchman had collected the money for his cattle, and was starting out for Swaledale on his way home to Scotland when a farmer and his son offered to show him a nearer way on to the moor. They took him through the hamlet of Newbiggin, half a mile east of Askrigg, and down a lonely lane which is a cul-de-sac, and here they murdered him. Then they discovered that a man and his sweetheart had been behind the wall all the time and had heard and seen everything. These two were promised a large sum of money if they kept the secret. The farmer's son galloped the Scotchman's horse over the moor, and it was found later at Tailbrig, at the head of Swaledale. They hid the body in a barn in Askrigg, and a few days later buried it on the moor.

It was known that the Scotchman had disappeared, and though the farmer and his son could not actually be found guilty, suspicion rested on them, especially as they suddenly had plenty of money. The man and his sweetheart who accepted the hush-money did not prosper. They married and took a farm, and bought a flock of sheep, but these were all drowned in a flood. When the man lay dying he was filled with remorse, and wanted to confess, but the murderers hung over him, saying: 'Tha mun dee hard, tha mun dee hard,' and never left him.

Years later the body was discovered on the moor by a man digging peat, and given a proper burial in Grinton churchyard. Tradition has it that a plaid, perfectly preserved in the peat, disclosed the identity of the Scotchman, and that the same plaid covers a sofa in

Swaledale to-day, but we have not seen the sofa or the plaid. An entry in the Grinton Parish Registers for the 18th of June 1797, of 'a person found by Ralph Harker buried in the peat moss in Whitaside . . .' may refer to the Scotchman. Recently a lady living in the house where the body was hidden, but who knew nothing of the story, saw a man in a grey plaid walk through the bedroom. So the tale of the murder of 'the Scotch lord,' added to occasionally by incidents such as these, is handed down from one generation to another.

Dalesmen still have a reverence for money. It offers to them something concrete in a world which is not too sure, for it is not made easily on the small farms. Two farmers met one day after one of them had been talking to a man who had been working out a family pedigree. 'Well, George,' said he, 'I finnd we're akin.' 'Are we?' said the other. 'Is there any brass at end on't?'

No change in its history or its people has robbed Askrigg of the moors behind it and the tracks across them. They are there always as an escape and an exhilaration. Returning along them, suddenly you see the town nestling under the hill. You welcome the restraint of its walls, knowing that behind them is the freedom of the fells.

Nappa Hall

CHAPTER XII

NAPPA HALL TO CARPERBY

THE road from Askrigg climbs steeply up Howgate, and runs on a terrace of the hill to Carperby, avoiding the hamlet of Newbiggin, and pausing at Nappa and Wood Hall.

The few scattered cottages of Nappa lie to the left, reaching up the hillside towards those other roads above Askrigg, but Nappa Hall is below on the other side, and is only seen by leaning over the wall. Its battlemented towers bring to mind the unsettled times in which it was built, when smaller houses as well as castles had to be protected. Once the home of great men, this is now a farmhouse. Built 1450–9, it is one of the few castellated houses left in Yorkshire. In a range of buildings to the south-east are parts of the first cottage which the hall replaced. Leland tells us that there was 'but a cotage or litle better house ontille Thomas Metcalfe began then to build,' and that it was 'communely caullid "No Castel."'

The main entrance leads through a porch to the lofty hall. The ground floor of the west tower, formerly the parlour, is now the kitchen of the farmhouse. Three rooms open from it, but only the floor of the lowest remains. A circular staircase running inside the four-foot thickness of the wall leads to them and the battlements.

There is glamour about this old house and the men who built and enlarged it, lived and entertained in it, and finally through extravagance and foolishness lost it. The family of Metcalfe came into Wensleydale in the twelfth century, when the name was Medecalf. For a hundred years not much is heard about them, then they began to gain the high positions in the dale. The main branch settled at Nappa in the fifteenth century. The estate, consisting of about four hundred acres, was given to James Metcalfe, who then lived at Worton, by Sir Richard Scrope of Bolton Castle, under whom he had fought at the Battle of Agincourt. His grandson, born the year after Nappa Hall was built, held many powerful offices; he was Master Forester of the Forests of Wensleydale, Raydale, and Bishopdale, High Sheriff of Yorkshire, and in 1525 was knighted by the king. He was also one of the king's commissioners, and held musters of men-at-arms, archers, and billmen for the Wapentake of Hang West on Middleham Moor. A list of these men drawn up for 1534 shows ninety-six of them to be Metcalfes, sixty-two from Bainbridge and Raydale.

After his death the family fortunes began to decline, though his son, Christopher, continued to live in the same extravagant fashion. To prove that it was possible to find three hundred men of the family of Metcalfe, Sir Christopher, when he was made High Sheriff of Yorkshire in 1556, attended the judges at York accompanied by three hundred of his kinsmen, riding white horses—these were probably greys, which were largely bred in the north at that time. The men who followed him were proud to belong to this great family which had grown into a clan.

But this almost princely dignity took more keeping up than the estate would allow, and at the death of Sir Christopher Metcalfe all but the Nappa estate and a few possessions near had gone. His grandson, Sir Thomas Metcalfe, the Black Knight of Nappa, was obliged to mortgage the estate and hall, though in his old age he was allowed to come back to the hall, where he died. His great-nephew, who died a bachelor in 1756, was described in his aunt's will as 'the last hopeful heir of the old ruinous house of Nappa.'

In the reign of Elizabeth, the Metcalfes, largely through their marriages, turned Protestant, and it was due to their influence that Roman Catholicism declined so rapidly in Wensleydale. They are not forgotten, for there are Metcalfes in nearly every village in the upper dale, and Metcalfes occupy Nappa Hall to-day.

The life round Nappa Hall is now solely the life of a farm. The courtyard echoes to the bleating of sheep in shearing or dipping time, and in the early evening cows stand patiently beside the barn in the lane waiting to be

milked. There is the view which the Metcalfes saw,
still peaceful and unspoilt, the river and the hills. They
too farmed this land, and grew on it more than is grown
to-day. The name, which in the thirteenth century was
'Nappay,' comes from the Old English, and means
'turnip field.'

The dalespeople have felt the dignity and awe of these
walls, and Nappa has been credited with several dis-
tinguished visitors: Mary Queen of Scots, who is said
to have spent a night here when she was a prisoner at
Bolton Castle; James I, who is believed to have been
carried across the Ure on the back of Sir Thomas Metcalfe's huntsman; and Sir Walter Raleigh, who is said
to have introduced crayfish into the River Ure. But
historical evidence does not prove these visits, and the
credit of introducing crayfish belongs to Sir Christopher
Metcalfe. Camden says: 'For hence runneth Ure downe
a maine, full of Creifishes, ever since Sir Christopher
Medcalfe in our remembrance brought that kinde of
fish hither out of the South part of England.'

These shellfish are now very plentiful in the Ure and
the smaller becks. They are like tiny lobsters, sandy
coloured, and when boiled they turn a deep red. Only
the two front claws and the tail are eaten. They are
often caught by throwing into the water a piece of tripe
or liver fastened to a length of string weighted with a
stone, and are then shaken off into a net. There is a
knack in catching them by hand as they nip with their
front claws, and although they walk forwards they swim
backwards. Watching them lurking under the rocky
edges of pools, you wonder how many generations of

crayfish have passed since their ancestors were put into the Ure in the sixteenth century.

Woodhall, a mile lower down, lies within Woodhall Park, an enclosure which was formerly a royal chase. The hamlet and hall where in the fifteenth century the Chief Forester of Wensleydale lived, lie on the other side of a woody hollow below the road. It is a hidden, forgotten little place, which yet has an air of contentment.

The slope on the left of the road beyond Woodhall, known as Hawbank, is dotted with lichen-covered trees, a relic of the old forest. Opposite it is Warren House, called after its warren of silver-grey rabbits. The warren stretches for eighty acres, and is surrounded by a high wall which goes several feet into the ground. It rises at one part to a knoll called Lady Hill, on the top of which is a group of fir trees. This is a landmark on both sides of the dale, specially conspicuous in the autumn, when it is covered with a golden carpet of bracken. Seeing it, you know that you have passed from the softer lower valley to the bleaker upper regions.

The baby rabbits are black, but by the time they are three years old they are beautifully marked with white hairs. Until the Russian Revolution the skins were sold at a high price to the Tsar of Russia. At that time poachers were severely dealt with; one owner put man-traps inside the wall, and a notice outside saying they were there. The pelts are still sold, a great number going to make felt hats. About every two years rabbits are imported from the Isle of Mull to improve the stock. Within the limits of the wall they are as free as wild rabbits, but they are given turnips and hay in winter.

Only in exceptionally bad snowstorms, when the drifts are as high as the walls, do wild rabbits make an entrance. If a hare happens to get in, the rabbits run it to death.

And so the road runs into Carperby, which consists of one main street with houses lining it on either side for over a mile. In the centre, the market cross, dated 1674, tells of the days when Carperby had a market, just as the name of the Wheatsheaf Hotel, a little further down, tells of the corn-growing days. This inn seems to have absorbed the spirit of Carperby with its mixture of bustle and repose. You may eat ham and eggs here from plates with deep pink borders, and in the middle coloured views of the beauty spots of the dale.

Carperby was and is a centre of Quakerism, and the meeting-house, itself a tall building, stands high above the road on the north side. The first meetings were founded by Richard Robinson in 1659, and Carperby was visited by George Fox on his preaching tours.

In spite of its air of lethargy it is a pleasant place. It seems sunk into the land from which it has only been able to claim this long street. Often as you pass through it you do not see a person. It wakes to life in the middle of fine mornings, when the school-children drill on the narrow green; or there is a moment's bustle when the rabbit van arrives, and the rabbit catchers come with pairs of rabbits packed closely together on sticks over their shoulders.

This part of the dale was the first home of Wensleydale sheep. The breed was started about 1838 with 'Blue Cap,' the son of a Leicester ram and a Teeswater ewe. At first they were called 'Mugs,' but a better name was wanted, and 'Wensleydales' was suggested by the late Mr. Thomas Willis of Carperby. Farmers talking to each other speak of them still as 'Mugs.' With their smooth, blue faces, and long, lustrous wool hanging almost to the ground, they present a contrast to the smaller, black-faced, mountain sheep. They are used largely for crossing with these, but neither they nor the cross-breeds can live on the highest fells. Wensleydale sheep have been sent to all parts of the world.

Mr. Thomas Willis also founded a herd of shorthorn cattle at Carperby in 1850, and won many prizes at the Royal Agricultural Shows. In the manor house are portraits of these animals, painted by A. M. Gauci, whose sisters put in the backgrounds. The cattle had enormous bodies and small heads, and when fattened for show weighed as much as twenty-seven hundredweight. One night in December a white cow was taken to the Bolton Arms Hotel in Leyburn ready to be sent by train to Smithfield. Morning found the market-place covered with ice, and it was thought that the cow would have to stay at home, as, weighing nearly a ton, it was doubtful whether, if she had fallen, she would ever have got up again. However, huge pads of sacking were tied on her feet and, with four men propping her up on each side, she slid down the market-place to the station. She won the Smithfield Supreme Championship, and her purchaser had her roasted whole on Boxing Day and given to the poor of Chelsea.

Customs change, but at Carperby you realize the centuries of farming which have gone on here, and the centuries which are to come. Cultivation ridges dating from Saxon times stretch down to it. A field on the south is still leased by three people who each plough a strip, leaving a ridge of grass between, a relic of the 'reins' of early agriculture.

Carperby lies at the foot of the fells. A lane starting in the centre comes out on to open moor with stretches of heather and bilberries, and the blue waters of Locker Tarn in the midst. A little way up, the lane is crossed by another going west to Askrigg over Oxclose, and east to Castle Bolton. It is a continuation of the jagging road which we left at Askrigg.

As we turned on to it, two men were digging a trench for water pipes which were to carry an extra supply for cattle, for Carperby had suffered in the drought of 1935. Water from springs on the moor is collected in large covered tanks, and laid to the villages and farms in narrow pipes, placed very little below the surface, and going through, not under, the streams. Quarrels have been known to result in the water pipe to a particular house being cut. Discussions of water supplies make much of the business at the Rural District Council meetings.

Now the path turns up the fell, and comes out on a natural plateau, a terrace of Nab End, the hill jutting into the valley here. It is worth while leaving the path and climbing to the summit for the view of the valley. You see also how it is divided into distinct hollows, which were once the beds of lakes left at the end of the Ice Age.

But the great interest of Nab End, like Addlebrough, lies in the evidence it gives of early occupation. Moors seem unchanging, and it is hard to believe that these hills have not always been lonely and deserted, inhabited only by birds, sheep, and rabbits; that once the climate was warm enough for men to live on them, and that these men were afraid of the lower country with its forests and bogs which they did not understand, or know how to drain. But signs of habitation are everywhere, not obvious—you could pass them by without noticing them; it is part of their fascination that they must be sought.

Almost on the summit of the hill, facing south-east, are remains of Bronze Age enclosures and hut dwellings of a village, dating from about 1000 B.C. Cultivated fields are recognized by little squares, bordered by loose stones. The people ploughed with small hand-ploughs, and stones were thrown to the side, and formed a wall. Larger enclosures were for goats. There are stone burial circles from which the sites of others near Askrigg can be seen, and which are themselves visible from more circles on the hills beyond Castle Bolton. Many burial circles must be lost in the heather, for you come across them unexpectedly, tracing them from one or two rocks showing on a bare piece. A perfect outline of a circle can be seen on the plateau below.

In the stony patches of the moor, and beside the gullies, there are traces of the work and habits of these people, flint arrow-heads, axes, and skin scrapers, and pieces of flint which have been chipped off in the making of them. There is something of the adventure of treasure hunting in searching for flints. The finding of the first piece with its smooth surface and the workings of the flintmaker on it is an excitement, and there is always the possibility that you will discover a perfect specimen. It is not a dignified proceeding, for unless your eyes are near the ground you miss them, so you balance in a flat position on tufts of grass or heather, and peer closely. With the finding of a piece comes a thought of the man who dropped it, the flintmaker. It is because he and others first thought to shape and use flint that we have reached our state of civilization. You glance below, and see the villages and farms of to-day, and perhaps a bus going up the valley, and realize how each life, short and often uneventful in itself, is part of the stream of life which never stands still.

On the plateau below, surrounding the stone circle, are the tippings of lead mines. The search for lead, which probably started with the first occupation of the hills, went on long after men had gone to live nearer the valley. Being later, the evidence of it, though now over-grown with grass and heather, is easier to find. Here are signs of lead mining of all periods: grooves in the scar made by 'hushing,' when the water was collected at the top and then turned down the hill, the shallow sinkings of the first miners, the bell-shaped shafts which the monks made, and later deeper shafts. Further along, the moor has been cut and piled into all shapes by the mine workings, outlines of dams are distinct, and parts of buildings remain.

There are ways down from Nab End to Nappa and Woodhall, but the main track goes along the slope of the fell, above the waterfall, Disher Force, and some woods, until it becomes a lane between walls and joins the road down to Askrigg, ending one of the loveliest walks in Wensleydale.

The Ure near Aysgarth

CHAPTER XIII

WORTON TO AYSGARTH

JUST below Howgate a smaller road turns from Askrigg to the other side of the valley, crossing the river by a wooden bridge which looks slender in comparison with the stone bridges of the Ure. You take it with the satisfactory feeling of having made a short cut in a district where often you must go miles to reach a village lying opposite.

In the turnpike days a chain was laid across this road where it enters the main road at Worton. Written as 'Werton' in Domesday Book, this is still pronounced 'Werton.' Its name, coming from the words *wyrt* and *tun*, means a township round a vegetable enclosure or garden. There is a hoariness about it. Many of the houses are dated. Worton Hall, with the date 1600, must be one of the oldest left in the dale; another at the corner has the inscription: '1729, Michael Smith, Mechanick, But He that built all things is God.' Michael Smith is said to have quarried and carted the stone, and built the house himself. Many are now country cottages, uninhabited for much of the year, so that its quietness is often that of emptiness, as though the place were hollow.

There was a bread riot here in 1757, resulting from the high price of corn. A quantity of corn was delivered at Worton for some gentlemen from Upper Wharfedale. The mob seized the greater part of it, and the owners had to go home with what little remained. One of those who escorted them on their way was Alexander Fothergill of Carr End, and he was attacked and injured as he returned the same night. A little later the mob rose again, and demanded money from householders in Raydaleside, Bainbridge, and Askrigg. They also took all the corn and meal from Middleham market at their own price. Several of them were caught and put into Richmond jail.

The main road down the valley follows the river, but an older road to Aysgarth turns up the hill to Cubeck, and passes through Thornton Rust. This runs along a ridge of the hill, like a gallery looking out upon the dale. Thornton Rust gives a similar sensation; no longer on the principal road, it seems to be a spectator at a distance. With its fine position, wide, open street, and the fells climbing up from it, it is an attractive place, but the altering and building of houses has taken away some of its character.

Before the Conquest Thornton Rust was probably owned by a man named Roschil, from whom the name 'Rust' comes. In 1301-2 John the Miller paid subsidy, but no mill remains, and only the site of its ancient chapel of St. Restitutus.

It is the Nonconformists who have developed here. A Calvinistic chapel at the east end is one of the few left in England. It was founded in 1827 by John Tomlinson, who endowed it with money to support a minister who was also to be schoolmaster. Attempts have been made to connect the church and school with other denominations, but Calvinists scattered over England have opposed it, and so every Sunday in Thornton Rust this creed is preached. The church occupies the top story of the building, and is reached by outside steps.

A school is still held in the room below with the minister for schoolmaster, though now only children up to ten years old are admitted. Entering it you feel to have stepped back several generations. Maps line the walls, and when we saw it there were open copy-books on the desks. Only simple subjects are taken, but the children learn them well. To step out from it is a little bewildering. Seeing the modern houses and gardens, you wonder if you have imagined the one-roomed school.

A house at the west end was also a chapel, built by a lady who disagreed on some point with the Calvinistic chapel, and started one of her own. The stone which went over the door is preserved, and its inscription reads: 'Jehovah my Banner. Particular Baptist Chapel. 1836.' It lasted only a few years, and was then made into a house. There was a pool in the stream behind the village where the 'Particular Baptists' were dipped for baptism. The loft of a barn behind this house was also used as a Wesleyan chapel. There was for long a custom of ringing a handbell at the centre and each end of Thornton Rust when an inhabitant died, as a public invitation to one member of each family to attend the funeral.

A mile away at the entrance to Aysgarth the road meets the main road again, getting a sudden view of the upper dale, with Lady Hill pointing the way to it. Just below, the road runs close to the river, and larches and beech trees growing on its grassy banks are reflected in the water. In the spring, swallows, their wings a deep blue in the sunshine, dart over it; there are forget-me-nots, and the smell of wild mint fills the air. After heavy storms the river floods here, and at these times the old road through Thornton Rust is very useful.

Aysgarth is built after the plan of a Norman village, but only the plan is left, and little that is old. Largely because of its famous waterfalls, it is the best known outside the dale of all the Wensleydale villages, and was popular with holiday-makers when less accessible places were unknown. People retired there to live; houses were rebuilt, and new houses erected. It has developed a slightly sophisticated look, but it is a pleasant village, a good place in which to live, and its air is the driest in England.

Much of its early importance arose from the fact that it was the parish for the whole of the upper dale, a parish extending westwards to the county boundary. Its church, built in Norman fashion away from the village, was the mother church.

L

A little way out of the village, beyond the roads which lead to Bishopdale, the road passes the Palmer Flatts Hotel, so called because a hospice for palmers or pilgrims once stood on the site. Towards the end of the nineteenth century it was frequented by wedding parties from all over the dale. The sanatorium opposite was formerly Aysgarth School, a preparatory school for boys, now moved to Newton-le-Willows. A road between the buildings leads down to the falls, and some of the finest scenery in the dale.

First a path turns off to the church in its beautiful position on the hill. Having been largely rebuilt in 1866, only the lower stages of the tower, carved stones, and two piscinas in the chapel remain to tell of the original late twelfth-century church. Fortunately its magnificent Perpendicular rood-screen was preserved, although moved to the south of the chancel. On the west face of the screen are remains of the rood-loft floor supported by fan vaulting, and with the initials 'H. M.' repeated twice on the east face. These initials, which are probably those of an unrecorded abbot of Jervaulx, occur again on a reading desk, which has also the initial 'W.' with a hazel tree and 'ton,' the rebus of William de Heslington, Abbot of Jervaulx. A beam in the chancel has the inscription 'A. S. Abbas anno Dm 1536'; the initials are those of Adam Sedbergh, the last abbot of Jervaulx. Probably because of these inscriptions, it has been concluded that the woodwork came from Jervaulx Abbey, carried, it is said, shoulder high by twenty men. But it is not of the type known to have existed in the abbey, and it is now thought to have been given by the monks of Jervaulx, to whom the church belonged, and to be the work of the Ripon carvers, of the kind they did for parish churches.

There is about Aysgarth church some feeling of its old importance and domination. It had the say over the churches higher up the dale, churches much poorer than itself, a position which its vicars sometimes exploited to their own advantage.

A flight of steps leads from the churchyard to Aysgarth bridge and the upper falls. The bridge, which was originally a packhorse bridge nine feet wide, was built with money left by James Sedgwick of Sedbergh in 1594 to 'the makinge of Aiskar Bridge.' You stand on tiptoe to peer over its parapet at the famous falls.

Until it reaches Aysgarth the Ure is a quiet river, winding for the most part through meadows, and adding nothing spectacular to the scenery. Its riotous spirits are concentrated into the stretch of its course below Aysgarth, where it drops two hundred feet, cutting through a rocky gorge in a series of magnificent waterfalls. The upper falls, passing over a broad semicircle of rock, are the best known. They are equally beautiful whether rushing as an angry torrent, going leisurely in innumerable small channels, or arrested in their flow by frost.

A gateway below the bridge leads to the bank of the river and the park-land which stretches from it. In the nineteenth century this open space above the fall was a favourite place for meetings and galas. To-day it makes a beautiful setting for the Aysgarth annual flower show, which, with its flower and tea tents, its sports in a neat ring, and its fancy dress parade, has something of the atmosphere of its predecessors.

The rolling country behind stretches beyond the railway to Bear Park, whose entrances are further along the road and on the Carperby road. The house, whose name comes from *beorg*, meaning hill, originally belonged to Marrick Priory in Swaledale. About 1458 it was leased to Brian Metcalfe, the 'Brian of Beare,' who is one of the heroes of Scott's poem, *The Felon Sow of Rokeby*. A carved stone inserted in the north wall was brought from Coverham Abbey by one of the Metcalfes. The present house is chiefly seventeenth century, but parts of a sixteenth-century building remain. It has old panelling, and some of the oak roof beams are fluted, and there is a powder room where the wigs were powdered.

Immediately below the falls, and adding to the picturesqueness of their surroundings, is Yore Mill, now used for grinding and storing corn. A mill was built here at the end of the eighteenth century for a cotton mill. Lord Torrington called it in his diary 'a Great flaring Mill,' and says that 'with the Bell Ringing and the clamour of the Mill all the Vale is disturbed.' Later it became a woollen mill, spinning yarn for the hand knitters. In 1853 it was burnt down, and rebuilt the following year. The sudden development of machinery left it with a great deal of stock unsold, but over seven thousand jerseys were sold to Italy to be used as the 'red shirts' of Garibaldi's army. In the early nineteenth century a school was held in a room in the mill by John Drummond, a noted mathematician. He was a descendant of the Earl of Perth, who lost his estates through participating in the Stuart rebellion, and, after hiding for a time in Bishopdale, settled in the district. No children learn their lessons in Yore Mill now, nor does the clamour of machinery destroy the peace of the valley, but the bell which called the people to work still hangs in its bell-cote on the roof.

A large pool in the river opposite the mill is used for washing sheep. The Middle Falls are just below. The Lower Falls, half a mile further down the river, are reached by a path through the Freeholders' wood, the only remaining portion of any size of the wooded part of the Forest of Wensleydale. The name Aysgarth means an open place marked by oaks. The wood is common land and, though paths are now cut through it, has an ancient look. Brambles and whitethorns creep round the hazel trees. This part of Wensleydale is famous for nuts—between here and Carperby there is one of the finest nut woods in Yorkshire. But hazel trees are plentiful all over the dale, and nuts are one of the most attractive features at harvest festivals.

The trees make an archway over the path which leads to the Lower Falls, whose roaring when the river is in flood is heard like thunder long before they are reached. The volume of water tossing and swirling is impressive, though there is terror in its fascination, but these falls are beautiful at all times. With the sound of them in your ears you return along the path. Dusk falls, and the gloom of the wood is intensified. For you the road lies just beyond, but you can realize here the difficulties of those early travellers in the forest, and their terror when night was coming on, of being lost.

West Burton

CHAPTER XIV

BISHOPDALE AND WALDENDALE

AYSGARTH gains in importance by its position above the junction of Bishopdale and Waldendale with the main dale. These two valleys join on the level land, and enter Wensleydale as one. They are a familiar sight from both roads up Wensleydale, running on either side of Wassett Fell, Waldendale, a narrow cleft in the hills, and Bishopdale, wide and dotted with woods, so like the lower dale that it seems a continuation of it. To carry out the illusion, Wensleydale, here where the change from the lower dale comes, takes one of its rare bends.

A road at the east end of Aysgarth turns to Thoralby in Bishopdale. From the top of the hill which runs down to it you see the whole of the dale, a wooded basin in the fells, changing comparatively little from one end to the other. It is 'bun' in,' as a dalesman described it, meaning 'bound in.'

The lower pastures are bordered by hedges, but there are still walls on the upper slopes. After the Ice Age this valley was a lake, its own melting ice being added to by the overflow from Semerwater over Thornton Mire. The thick drift which the lake left behind, reaching here an unusual height up the fells, has made the land rich and fertile and flat in the bottom; through it the Bishopdale Beck cuts a sluggish way. In Saxon and Norman times the dale was a chase, a favourite pasture ground for deer, who preferred it to the wilder valleys.

Thoralby, the first village, lies in a kind of backwater away from the main roads, quiet and unspoilt. It gazes from its beautiful situation on the south side of the valley over the curving slopes of Penhill and Wassett Fell. Its name means 'Thorold's farm,' and in the same way Bishopdale is 'Bisceop's valley.' It is a scattered village. Unexpected roads and lanes branch off in all directions, but each has a purpose; one called Gooseberry Lane leads to a ford across the beck; another climbs to a track over the fell. Heaning Gill, a wooded ravine at the end of the village, has a beautiful waterfall, appropriately called the Silver Chain. The mill, which at the foot of a steep hill makes an attractive entrance at the south end, was working as a corn mill in 1857.

There is a chapel, but in this village you miss a church. In the fourteenth century there was a church, known as the 'Great Chapel of Thoralby,' in which Mary de Neville of Middleham founded a chantry in 1316. It became a ruin after the chantry was dissolved in 1548, and nothing remains of it except the name of a field, Chapel Close, which marks its site.

An old and unoccupied house, now used for storing timber, at the west end, may have been used for religious services, for there are texts on the walls under the top layer of plaster which is peeling away. The house has the air of a hall, but within memory it has had no name. Above the doorway of the porch are the initials M.S., and the date 1704. There is a story in the village that treasure is buried in the house. An old man dreamt that he saw a black teapot filled with gold sovereigns under the floor, and at times flagstones have been removed to search for it. In the porch hangs a witch stone, a relic of the days when these stones with holes through them were hung in houses and stables to prevent misfortune; it adds to the mystery of the house.

Down Westfield Lane at the end of the village is Littleburn Hall, where Matthew, the fourth Lord Rokeby, lived. A bridge crossing the beck to it was built as a memorial to the Duke of Wellington, and dedicated to him in a Latin inscription, which also states how dangerous the beck can be in times of flood.

Opposite the old house, standing back from the road beyond a cobbled yard, is the George Inn, which has a retiring air, but is a vital part of the village. There is no village hall here, and it is in the inn that the weighty affairs of the dale are discussed. In the parlour are pictures painted by the son of the landlord when he was a boy: one of the inn with a horse and wagonette standing on the cobbles brings back the atmosphere of the days before cars; another shows the Bolton farm wagon with its gay colours. He painted without any teaching, sometimes from memory when ill in bed, but there is vigour in the pictures.

Once a week a bus comes into Thoralby to take the people to Leyburn market. It is a large red bus, but it is treated with as little ceremony as the most homely country affair. No crowds wait for it; it creeps down into what seems a sleeping village. Presently a figure appears in a doorway, and the driver calls out: 'City's very quiet this morning.'

'Aye,' says the man, 'we've nobbut just gitten up,' and shuts the door again.

It looks as though the bus had had a useless journey, but at eleven o'clock, the hour at which it is supposed to leave, a man appears, carrying a sack, and gradually the bus fills. A woman has a basket from which the feet of a large cockerel protrude into the gangway, catching upon each new passenger, until someone has the idea of turning the feet inwards. There is an air of holiday and joviality, and every little incident is enjoyed. The progress of farming is noted on the way, how Jack is getting on with his manuring, and Ted has bought some new calves. Then someone remarks: 'We've gitten teu't,' and baskets and bundles are gathered together. The same group waits the return bus, often ready long before it appears; a little tired, and some of them a little merry, they arrive home in time for the evening milking.

Market-day ends with discussions in the bar of the George Inn. Each day brings its own experiences and reminiscences, but the subject seldom varies, for this is a farming community. Sheep and lambs, cows and milk, but here cows take the first place. 'T 'best bagged coo i' Leyburn market,' is a subject to be treated with respect. The farmers take a pride in their cows, and good ones are remembered for a lifetime.

A farmer tells how he bought what looked a very fine cow, and was driving it home, very proud of his purchase, when he met a man coming the other way. The man spoke before he reached him.

'Seea ye 've gitten 'er,' he said.

'Aye,' said the farmer; 'do ye ken 'er?'

'Aye, I deu.'

'Whya, is ther owt wrang wi' 'er? Ye 'd best tell me.'

'Whya, she 's hard.'

'Hard?'

'Hardish.'

'An' I fun' it were true,' says the farmer. 'I could milk all t' coos in t' time it teuk me to milk that yan.'

One winter's morning, as we sat in the low room at the George Inn, someone came out to sweep the steps and cobbles. There had been a slight fall of snow in the night, and now it was crisp and powdery, glistening in the brilliant sunlight. There was a clatter of clogs on the cobbles, and a voice said: 'Grand mornin'!'

'Aye,' was the answer.

The sweeping continued; then there were more footsteps.

'Grand mornin'!'

'Grand!'

More sweeping, more footsteps.

'Grand mornin'!'

'Aye.'

And so the dialogue continued. The 'Grand mornin''
never varied, and it seemed an opportunity to take the
walk over Stake Fell to Bainbridge. We turned up
Haw Lane, a grassy track near the west end of the
village, generally spoken of as 't' high rooad.' The
grazing on the lane is let by auction, about thirty
shillings a year being bid for it. For many years an old
lady grazed three milk cows on it, and trudged up it
twice a day to milk them. Haw Lane merges into
a path.

That morning the snow had drifted, leaving a ridge
down the trunks and branches of the trees and the bars
of gates. It was a scene in clear-cut black and white.
In the meadow in front of Gayle Ing Farm, a young
bull, out for exercise, lowered his head and came towards
us, then suddenly changed his mind and galloped away.
Hares had made numbers of tracks in the snow. The
hunt seldom troubles to come so far out, and the land is
overrun with hares. The farmer has counted thirty as
he walked up from Thoralby. He is not allowed to
shoot them, although four hares will eat the equivalent
of one sheep.

The isolated dale houses are usually occupied by young
people. The high moor farms being the least expensive
to rent, a man will take one for his first, moving when he
can afford a bigger rent. So the high farms get changing
tenants. In many ways this works well; the people live
in the out-of-the-way places while they are young and
can stand the walking. On the other hand, it means
that the children have to walk long distances to school
in all weathers.

From Gayle Ing the path goes over the fells, and presently the Raydale valley appears, distant and mystical, and the path becomes a lane again as it nears the farm at Carpley Green. As we returned an Alpine glow faintly coloured the summit of Penhill. The warm red sky paled quickly, and passed from yellow to a clear, cool green. Then darkness came, and the stars and the rising moon in their turn lit valley where winter is as beautiful as summer. As we neared the village it began to snow steadily, deadening all sound. Next morning the snow and frost had vanished, and the land was soft and green again.

On the opposite side of the valley is the village of Newbiggin, which Thoralby people say is on the 'money side,' while theirs is on the 'sunny side.' It is a fascinating place, either from a distance or near to, running along a straight road under Wassett Fell. Its very common name means 'new buildings,' but many of the houses are seventeenth century, and there is a feeling of age about it, as if long ago something had stopped its growth. A path runs from it past Forelands Farm and over Wassett Fell into Waldendale. A road turns from the village to Street Head Inn on the main road up Bishopdale.

As you start up it a busy twittering comes from a group of trees as numbers of long-tailed tits move with swift, sharp flights from one branch to another, hanging mostly upside down from the branches, intent on picking insects. A field near by seems a dull fawn colour as hundreds of fieldfares feed there. Seeing you they rise into the air, not simultaneously, but as if something were sweeping them off, and all the time uttering a peculiar clucking noise.

A school on the roadside was built, when education became compulsory, for the children of the scattered farms where there were usually large families. The schoolmaster lived for a few weeks at a time at each farmhouse. Now a car comes up the dale, and fetches the children to West Burton to school, and brings them back at night, and so modern progress rolls them on to a more sociable life than the older children knew.

The farmhouses are more than rough cottages. Many retain their stone window mullions—West Newhouse, dated 1635, has six, and in spite of its name is one of the oldest houses in the dale. Old maps give names for the barns attached to them.

In Foss Gill, past Scar Top House, there are two fine waterfalls. The pool formed by the higher one is used for washing sheep. Sheep are seldom washed nowadays —with compulsory dipping it is no longer necessary, but washed wool fetches a higher price, and the practice is kept up in Bishopdale. The lower fall comes over a projecting ridge like Hardraw, and it is possible to walk behind it. When the beck is too full to cross, the shepherd takes his sheep that way; sending his dog behind, he picks up one sheep in his arms, and the rest follow.

The road now climbs the famous Kidstones Pass into Wharfedale, meeting at the top the Stake Pass from Stalling Busk. There is not the feeling of unbroken moorland on this summit. Substantial walls are everywhere, meadows creep up to the ridge of fells across Wharfedale, and turning back you see the greenness of

Bishopdale. On the fells a mile to the east there is a small, dark patch, which seems merely a heap of stones, but when you get nearer shows to be the gabled end of a ruined building. On one of the stones is the date 1758 and H.H. It is given on old maps as Cannons, Castle Hill, and is called locally Cannons Castle.

It is an easy walk down the dale with Bolton Castle before you in the distance, now sinking into the hill, now gleaming in the sunshine. Bishopdale draws you back into its pleasantness and prosperity. Presently the road passes the Thoralby road again, and runs on a ridge of the hill to West Burton.

West Burton lies at the junction of Bishopdale and Waldendale, where Wassett Fell which divides them gives way to the valley, and belongs equally to the two dales, although it is actually on Walden Beck. It is a beautiful village, with houses climbing up both sides of a hilly green. Almost a show place, it is saved from sophistication by an inn planted on the village green on one side and a cottage on the other. You wonder if they like their conspicuous positions or would rather step back into the rows and live arm-in-arm with their neighbours. The village cross beside the inn was first erected in 1820, and restored in 1889. The stocks near it are modern.

A street parallel with the green brings back the more ancient atmosphere of West Burton, once a place with a customary market. The Walden Beck flows at the north end, and here there is a waterfall, formed when melting glaciers deepened the valley, and the beck had to cut through a gorge to reach the lower level. Below the

village a packhorse bridge crosses the beck, starting a
road which runs along the low slopes of Penhill to
Middleham Moor. Flanders Hall lies just below, and
beyond it is Edgeley, once the home of Mrs. Elizabeth
Montagu, the essayist, who held meetings of the 'Blue-
Stocking Club' at her London home.

The road up Waldendale starts at the top of West
Burton, and goes on the west side above the beck. The
valley does not display its beauty all at once: round each
twist and bend it gives a fresh delight. Only scattered
farms dot the hillsides, and the few plantations are small
and sparse compared with those in Bishopdale, but it is
the gravity of the valley which makes its charm. There
is no suggestion of a main way about the road up it,
made not for outsiders to travel through, but for the
people of the dale.

As you go along it you see that against the wall of a
barn a gamekeeper has hung the stoats and rats he catches,
and their grim warning adds intensity to the valley.
Heaps of manure dot the fields. The carting and spreading
of this is one of the farmers' principal jobs during
autumn and winter; only so can he prevent his meadows
and pastures from going back to moorland, and on it his
crops of hay depend. Where the road dips to a hollow
a youth drives a low cart up the slope. He whistles as
he rides, and the cheerful sound, added to the ring of
the horse's hoofs, breaks the silence strangely.

Now the road passes a school building, closed like the
Bishopdale one, except for Sunday services, church one
week and chapel the next. Now there are open fields on
one side, and grazing horses regard you indifferently, not

troubling to move. A bracken stack perches jauntily on the hill. The road crosses the beck by a sturdy bridge, and mounts the other side a rougher track. Two houses across it, Routon Gill Farms, seem to be the last in the valley, but the road goes on, the hills still overlapping, shutting out the end. Buckden Pike seems an unsurmountable barrier. An empty cottage by the roadside was for years the home of an old man who lived by himself. He used to talk to the children as they came from school, and they called him 'Uncle.' When he died the farm was joined to another, but the tenants speak of the rent for it as 'rent for Uncle's.'

Suddenly the road is by the beck again. Along it are ash trees, beautiful alike in leaf or winter nakedness, and between them peep the cottages and barns of the hamlet of Walden Head. A white house across the beck seems the house of dreams. The fells shut it in, but there is no feeling of clinging to them, Walden has a valley's characteristics. It is not what you expect to find at the end of this dale with its reckless beauty.

The first feeling of a community here becomes modified, for the houses across the beck are unoccupied. But their desertion is comparatively recent, and they have not yet the appearance of ruins. They are on the sunnier side of the valley, but only a footbridge leads to them, and when the beck is full carts and cattle cannot cross. One is known as 'T' Aud Wife,' because a widow with nine or ten children once lived there.

From Walden Head you can follow the beck to its start, and go over the moor to Starbotton in Wharfedale, or climb Buckden Pike to Buckden, or Tor Mere to

Kettlewell. The people do not think of a large dale, but of the villages in it, when they think of the country on the other side of the hill. We asked a girl how long it would take to reach Wharfedale.

'Mother,' she called into the house, 'wheea 's Wharfedale?'

'Somewheea ower Kettlewell way,' was the answer.

From the first road bridge there is a way back to West Burton on the east side of the beck. This starts as a path with stone slabs bridging the tiny gills, but at the first farmhouse it becomes a lane. Now a signpost points the way to Coverdale and Nidderdale. Past a ruined smelt mill, a reminder of the vanished lead-mining industry, is Cote Farm, where another track goes over to Coverdale, and makes a good starting point for climbing Penhill. Then the road wanders into West Burton again, and it is as though you had dreamt of the valley behind with its loveliness and appeal.

M

Bolton Castle

CHAPTER XV

THORESBY AND CASTLE BOLTON

A FORD with a name other than the place to which it belongs catches your interest. You feel that it must have had some special quality to be singled out. Slapestone Wath, meaning 'the ford of the slippery stones,' is one of the few which have retained the names given them by the Norsemen. It is reached down a lane which turns towards the river opposite the lowest road to Bishopdale. Slapehow, one of the first dwellings of the Knights Templars in Wensleydale, is thought to have been near this ford.

An ancient track, known as 'Wattery Loan' (Water Lane), connects with the ford on the north of the river. This also is no longer used, its surface is furrowed by water, and its uncut hedges have grown and met at the top. Made to accommodate packhorses and cattle, it is so narrow that from the fields on either side it looks to be merely an overgrown hedge. The spirit of its early users seems caught in the tangled trees. It leads to the site of the ancient village of Thoresby.

A settlement was probably founded here by the Norsemen who gave it its name, meaning 'Thor's Farm.' They chose their site well, on secluded, wooded land, typical of the banks of the Ure in this part of Wensleydale, but raised above the river, away from the danger of flooding. It was a village in the Middle Ages, by which time it had become the home of a family who took their name from it. John de Thoresby, who was born here, became Lord Chancellor, and was Archbishop of York from 1354 to 1373. He gave the magnificent choir and Lady Chapel to York Minster. Ralph Thoresby, the antiquarian and historian, is said to have descended from this family.

Nothing now remains of the village but uneven mounds, which are obviously foundations of houses, covered by earth and overgrown with grass, and quite different from the rounded mounds of glacial drift. Ancient pottery, a flint arrow-head, and two hunting knives have been found; and the name of one of the fields, Chapel Bottoms, suggests that there was a church here. Numbers of burnt stones now built into the boundary walls were probably blackened by smoke. Nothing is heard of Thoresby after the fourteenth century. It is the most interesting of the lost villages of Wensleydale, for, knowing something of it, you can reconstruct the place for yourself, and that is its fascination. The name is retained in two farmhouses, High and Low Thoresby, nearer the road.

The lane enters the main road on the north side, near West Bolton Farm. Following Beldon Beck at the west of the farmhouse, you come upon a small stone circle. It is probably a Bronze Age burial circle, though, unlike that on Nab End, its separate stones show a few feet above the ground. It lies so near the bank of the beck that some of the stones have fallen in. Perhaps because of its secluded position, imagination plays on this ancient relic, and you understand why it is called locally the Druid's Temple.

One of the most interesting features in this part of the dale is the series of broad terraces on the hillsides, signs of Saxon strip cultivation. These terraces are seen on many of the lower slopes, but they are nowhere so numerous as on this piece between Carperby and Castle Bolton. Their presence indicates the site of an early settlement, which, in most cases, is that of the present village. Each man had so many strips to cultivate, and these were changed every three years, so that each got his share of good or bad soil. On the level land the strips were divided by ridges of grass left unploughed, and were called 'reins'—a relic of this system remains in the field at Carperby. On these hillsides the strips were made into terraces and the sides firmly built with stone. They were usually a furlong in length, and wide enough for four oxen to pull the plough. They are called lynchets, and run generally from east to west, though the direction was often altered to suit the lie of the land. They were not cut as now by walls. At the end of the fifteenth century and the beginning of the sixteenth, as the land between the villages began to be cultivated, the system was gradually discontinued. The hilly land would then be used as meadow or pasture, and the shape of the terraces is left. The level land being still ploughed, the 'reins' were destroyed. All that remains here are shallow waves on the fields, the 'rigg and furr' of later ploughing.

Signs of 'rigg and furr' on the moor show where attempts have been made to cultivate the higher flat land. These were not successful, for the corn did not ripen soon enough. Even on the lower land there are tales of corn being cut in November, and of sheaves being brought in to dry by the fireside. The cultivation terraces stretch to Bolton Castle, which itself probably followed the manor house of an earlier village.

Bolton Castle dominates this part of the dale. Seen from the moors, from up or down or across the valley, it is a focus on the long northern ridge. A path across the fields past West Bolton and Castle Bank Farms comes out at the castle. From the narrow road which turns up to it from the main road you see it in another aspect, softened by trees. But from most sides it stands out bare and unhidden, though always its grim walls achieve beauty, as well as strength. Its importance seems still to influence the valley, for in the distance it has not the look of a ruin.

In this strategic position the Scropes built their castle, one of the finest examples in England of a fourteenth-century fortified palace. Its four corner towers with two smaller towers on the north and south sides surround a rectangular courtyard. Started in 1379, it took eighteen years to build, and each year cost a thousand marks, making the total cost twelve thousand pounds, a tremendous sum for those days. The oaks in the neighbourhood were not large enough to make the heavy beams, and timber was brought from the Forest of Engleby in Cumberland by 'dyvers Draughts of Oxen to cary it from Place to Place till it cam to Bolton.' It came along the old road which we have followed above Lunds, Askrigg, and Carperby.

The entrance to the castle was at the east side through a vaulted arch, guarded at each end by a portcullis, and with a porter's lodge on the south. It opened to the courtyard, from which there were four doorways into the castle, each again guarded by a portcullis. Thus before an entry could be made three barriers had to be passed. This entrance is not used now, and farm carts and implements stand under the arch, but you can look through the iron gateway into the courtyard, and imagine an arrival there with all its caution and ceremony. The present entrance is by a flight of steps on the west side.

The castle was built by Richard, Lord Scrope, whose family had held land in Bolton from early in the thirteenth century. He was knighted at the Battle of Neville's Cross in 1346, but the family as a whole were famous as lawyers rather than soldiers. The father and uncle of Richard, Lord Scrope, both became Chief Justices of the King's Bench, and he himself was Chancellor of England in 1378. He was also Keeper of the Great Seal, and is notable for having refused to put the seal to a foolish order made by Richard II.

The Scropes were famous men, but their significance

at Bolton is overshadowed because the castle once held as prisoner Mary Queen of Scots. She was imprisoned here from 13th July 1568 to 26th January in the following year, under the custody of the ninth Baron Scrope, at that time Governor of Carlisle, and Sir Thomas Knollys. And because she lived here for those six months the interest of the castle centres on her, on the rooms she occupied, and what she did there. She lived with a certain amount of state, bringing with her a retinue of forty servants, more than half of whom had to be billeted in cottages in the village. Sir George Bowes supplied extra hangings and beddings from his own house, and Queen Elizabeth sent household utensils and other 'necessaries incident to dinners.' There was a weekly supply of venison, and she was also allowed to hunt.

Her apartment was in the south-west tower, a large retiring room, with steps leading out of it to her bedroom. A niche in the fireplace of the room was where her glass of wine would be placed to warm. Here Sir Francis Knollys taught her English, and she called him her good schoolmaster. On 1st September she wrote her first letter in English, and addressed it to him. Sir Christopher Norton was in attendance on her here, and he told in his confession when he was being tried for high treason how one day he was watching Lord Scrope and Sir Francis Knollys playing chess while the queen knitted before the fire. Looking round and finding that her servants had gone to their meal, she called to him to come and hold her work. A little later Sir Francis looked up and saw them, and asked his captain if Sir Christopher ever watched. 'Sometimes,' said the captain; and Sir Francis commanded that he should watch no more lest the queen should make him a fool.

She scratched her name on a window pane in this room, but the glass was accidentally broken while being moved to Bolton Hall. There is also a legend that during her imprisonment she escaped from the window, and reached Leyburn Shawl, where she was captured at a place ever since called 'The Queen's Gap.' It is argued in support of this tradition that the queen was hurried away from Bolton at a very inconvenient time of the year, but this was more probably because of the visit of Lady Scrope's brother, the Duke of Norfolk, who had proposed marriage to her, hoping to ascend the throne. It was while she was at Bolton that the question of her complicity in the murder of her husband, Darnley, was tried. You wonder as you step into the main banqueting hall on the north side whether Queen Mary went on to the balcony above, from which the ladies watched the banquets, or attended the chapel of St. Anne on the south side, dedicated in 1399. For less favoured prisoners there was a dungeon, a dismal place entered by a trap in the roof.

Water could be drawn from the well at the east end of the hall to an upper room, and could also be poured down a narrow outlet into the courtyard. The brewhouses and bakehouses were in the south, and here parts of ovens and vats remain, and shoots from the floor above, probably for malt. The heating arrangements were advanced for that period; whilst in most buildings fireplaces were still being made in the centre of the room, the smoke going through a lantern in the roof, at Bolton there were chimneys. You can climb to the south-west tower and look down to the village, minute and far away, and you may see a pair of sparrow-hawks swoop with an eagle-like movement to their nest on another tower.

The castle was garrisoned for Charles I against the parliamentary forces, and held by Colonel Chaytor of Croft until 5th November 1645, by which time the besieged were reduced to eating horseflesh; in 1647 it was made untenable. The north-east tower, which had been weakened in the siege, fell during a storm on 19th November 1761.

The west entrance leads down a passage into a museum. Here are the old forest horn and a Roman millstone from Bainbridge, a piece of lead pipe from Fors Abbey, and Roman and British articles, swords and arrow-heads, found in various parts of the dale. A tour of the castle starts in the museum, and ends in the kitchen of the caretaker's house. This sudden turning into a homely living room is almost an anticlimax, but within living memory there were several cottages in the castle. In 1858 a tinker and a glazier had workshops there, and sheet lead was cast in the vaults. To-day one of the large rooms forms the village hall.

As we crossed from the castle to the church a hare lolloped undisturbed along the quiet road between them, and disappeared into the field beyond. In another position the little church of St. Oswald would be a normal size for the village, but, standing close under the castle walls, it seems a toy building, and for most of the

day the sun is hidden from it. A church was founded
here in the twelfth century, but the present building is
Decorated, of much the same date as the castle. It is
aisleless, with no chancel arch, but three corbels east of
the nave have evidently held a rood-loft. In Bolton
museum there is a serpent, an old wind instrument,
which a Redmire lady remembers her grandfather
playing as part of the band which supplied the music in
the church. Probably one of the last instances of public
apology took place here. A woman had slandered
another, and the apology was demanded by the whole
village. During the service she had to walk up and down
the aisle, and at the end of it make her apology, which
she did in rhyme.

The village creeps along the ridge from the castle, as
if it still shared in its protection, but it has enough
individuality not to be swamped by it. A green where
horses and donkeys graze borders the road on both sides.
The houses lining it do not face each other, but all look
the same way, as if neither side wanted to lose the view
over the valley—the lower row drops down a little not to
hide it from the rest. The name 'Castle Bolton' dis-
tinguishes it from the other Boltons in the country. It
is the first village in the dale on the Bolton Hall estate,
and forms with Redmire and Preston-under-Scar a group
of villages which owed much of their prosperity to the
lead and coal mines on the moors behind.

Many of the miners rented smallholdings, so that
these places stayed farming communities, making the
industry which invaded them fit their lives instead
of spoiling and altering them. The lead mines were

chiefly on the north side of the valley, and it is on this side that most of the industries have flourished. Even the early Britons seem to have confined their flint making to the north, and merely to have hunted and reared their flocks on the south.

Life in the mining days was not easy. Wages were low, and there were no luxuries; gulls (oatmeal porridge), brown bread, and havercake were the chief food. Sometimes a little white flour was obtained by putting brown flour through a fine sieve, called a 'temse,' and this was made into dumplings or a small white loaf, but white bread was often considered so precious that it was cut into slices and dried, and used to make bread and milk. A few people would join and buy a cow at Middleham Moor Fair in November, and this they would kill, cut up, and pickle, for the winter's supply of meat.

At that time donkeys were much used for carting, and small herds of them used to be put to graze on the moor. If the miners came across them on their way to work, they would mount them, and ride them to the mines a mile or two away, and leave them to find their way back. A Bolton woman, named Bella Johnson, kept a team with which she used to cart coal from Bishop Auckland. This is one of the few places where the use of them has survived; there is generally one peering under a gate as you pass.

From the seats on the green you can watch the simple life of the village which has survived the life of the castle and the mines. A young man wheels a barrow along the road, and vanishes to reappear triumphantly with a newly born calf curled awkwardly inside. Now a man comes riding a donkey with a back-can fastened on either side of the saddle; he is bringing the milk from the cow pastures behind the village. Others follow, some with cans in carts, some with back-cans slung on their backs. These cans, sometimes called 'budgets,' are curved inwards on one side to fit the back, and whether a man or a donkey carries them, are a picturesque sight. The people are still chiefly smallholders, keeping one or two cows on the common pasture. The large farms lie outside the village.

There is no road beyond the castle; the road at the west turns down to the main highway again. The village owes its peace and quiet to the fact that there is no real way through. The narrow lane at the east end crosses the wooded ravine of Bolton Gill, and joins the moorland road from Grinton in Swaledale to go steeply down into Redmire.

Redmire's Oak

CHAPTER XVI

REDMIRE

WHILE Castle Bolton sits bravely on the hill, Redmire snuggles under it. They are like two sisters with lots cast in different surroundings, yet remaining great friends. Though so different, they share each other's amusements, joys, and sorrows. Redmire is in harmony with its position; the hills and woods and river seem to have accepted it as part of themselves. Its houses, at first scattered, draw gradually together, and open out at the village green. The market cross is new, but stands on its original steps. Near it is the Redmire oak, so old that its branches have to be propped up, and it is fenced off for protection.

The people congregate on the green on Saturday afternoons in summer before the cricket matches, and discuss the chances of the local team as each new member arrives. A car packed with most of the opposing team arrives noisily and parks on the green. Then all wander slowly to a field behind the Bolton Arms Inn; here cricket is played on one half, and a lynchet forms a convenient raised platform for the spectators on the other.

At the end of September the annual feast, a picturesque remnant of the old Redmire Feast, is held on the green. The show people come in old motor buses, and within an hour of their arrival they are camped on the green with their cans and belongings grouped round them, as if they had been settled there for days. In this setting the stalls with their striped awnings have not the taw-dry effect of fairs in a town, and the colours seem to express gaiety and fun.

In the eyes of the old people the glory of the fair has gone. The stalls and roundabouts filled the green, and it was the holiday of the year; people who had left the village came back, and every house was full. Houses were cleaned down for the occasion, and fresh curtains hung at every window. One of the chief events was a donkey race which started at the top of the hill to the east and ended at the town hall, and for which there was a prize of a bridle. One year a donkey which was 'a real good 'in, terble good for gallopin',' came first in the race into Redmire, but when it saw the unusual crowd, it stopped and refused 'to face the company.' Quoiting competitions were another feature. This game is still played, one part of the green near the old oak being reserved for practice. Another game was wallops, in which skittles were put on the ground, and a stick thrown at them to knock down as many as possible. There was also a greasy pole to climb, and the prize of a pig for whoever managed it. On one occasion when the winner had fattened and killed his pig and hung it up to dry, the rope broke and every bit of the ham and bacon went wrong. The tragedy is remembered vividly.

During the feast week the young men of the village dressed up and went from house to house begging for cheesecakes; they also had a bottle and a feather which they would hold out, saying: 'We've come to oil the clock,' and people would put something in the bottle. Though most of the glamour and excitement has gone, it is typical of Redmire that it still keeps up its feast when others have died out.

The name Redmire comes from the Old English *hreod*, reed, and *mere*, a lake. There used to be a lake on the low land at the south of the village, but it developed into a reedy swamp, and was drained about a hundred years ago. Here you have passed completely into the lower dale with many trees and a few ploughed fields appearing, where the valley begins to count more than the fell. The dialect too has changed; the 'card' (cold) of the upper dale has become 'caud,' the 'fells' have become 'moors,' and the people are gentler and more tolerant. In the village itself, in its tales and legends, the old mingles with the new in a fascinating medley. Many customs have died out so recently that they are still fresh in the minds of the people.

Redmire, like Bolton, was chiefly inhabited by miners. Thomas Maude, who wrote a poem on Wensleydale in

1780, began the verse on Redmire with 'Of Redmire's mining town how shall we sing?' The village retains the feeling of a community which lead mining seemed to encourage, of every one working on a common interest. It was not spoilt by the mines, which were out of sight on the moor.

Important as the lead-mining industry was, it was claimed, even in its most prosperous days, that more butter, cheese, and bacon in weight was exported from Wensleydale than lead. The dairy on the hill behind, now a branch of the Cow and Gate factory, often makes in the weeks before Christmas a ton of cheese a day, another proof of how these new dairies are continuing and increasing what was always a large industry.

The town hall was built for the old Dale Volunteers, formed by Lord Bolton during the Napoleonic War. The Volunteers were to know if they were needed by the lighting of a beacon on Penhill, which in its turn was to receive a beacon from Roseberry Topping. One day the heather on Roseberry Topping caught fire, and the warden on Penhill, thinking it was the beacon, lit his own. The Wensleydale Volunteers were well on their way to Thirsk before the mistake was discovered. At the roll-call at Middleham there were only two absent. One was John Alderson, whose wife answered for him: 'Jack 's i' t' pit, but ah 'se here, and he wad be here teu if he knew.' The Volunteers were thanked for their loyalty by both houses of Parliament.

Inhabitants can remember corn being ground in the ruined mill beside the beck in the village, where there was a horse whee¹. Lightfoot Hall, a manor house in the middle of the village, is now a row of cottages; one has an original fireplace and the great cellars are below. It is supposed to be haunted by two members of the Lightfoot family who come out on to the wall, one combing her hair, and the other making butter.

Eighty years ago one of the two shops in Redmire was also a school, kept by a lady in a house which now has a neat little garden open to the road. The shop was in the living-room where the school was also held, except in the summer when a tiny room opening out of it was used. Lessons had to stop when a customer arrived. The schoolmistress had a daughter who worked at one of the Thoresby farms, and received as part of her wage a pint of milk a day. The cream was skimmed off this, and once a week while she gave her lessons the lady churned it into butter.

This was not thought peculiar. The people were obliged to be frugal, even made a virtue of it. One girl shocked them all by buying two pictures for her one-roomed house when she was married. Another girl went to a farm for a month to help with the hay-making, and received at the end a guinea for wages. 'Now doan't spend it fondly,' said the farmer, as he gave it to her. She really meant to follow his advice, but the next day a travelling pedlar came round, and she spent it all on a tea-service. Her daughter, now an old lady, owns it proudly, and blesses her burst of extravagance.

In many dale villages there were men with second sight, and it used to be the custom for them to go and sit in the churchyard on St. Mark's Eve, when they would see the

N

spirits of the people who were going to die during the year walk into the church. A sexton at Redmire saw the doomed ones, not only on St. Mark's Eve, but any time in his dreams, which were never known to be wrong.

The people who until recently kept up the old customs and beliefs have also kept alive some of the stories which used to be told round the firesides. There is the feeling of an ancient ballad in the tale of the farmhouse on Tewfit Howe, a hill behind Redmire whose name means 'Thufa's hill.' Nothing of it remains except the story. It tells how the master and mistress had gone to Redmire church, leaving a servant girl alone in the house. Presently two robbers appeared, and one knocked at the door. The girl opened it, although she had been warned not to do so, and the man pushed his way in, and sat down in the kitchen. But the kitchen was hot after the cold air outside, and in a few minutes he fell asleep with his head on the back of the chair and his mouth open. The girl had her suspicions about him, and she took a mug of hot broth from a pan on the fire, and poured it down his throat. The other robber, after waiting a time for his mate, climbed on to the roof, and shouted down the chimney: 'Hey, Tommy! Ho, Tommy! Is ta within?' at which the maid called back: 'Hey, Tommy! Ho, Tommy! He's scalded to t' skin!'

A narrow lane, which turns at the south-east corner towards Wensley, runs for part of the way by a beck. Here where houses and people are forgotten, and the meadows and trees envelop you, Redmire church stands alone, a humble building without tower or spire, only a bell-cote. The church is Norman. As you approach

you see that its plainness is relieved by the south doorway, which has zigzag on the arch and diaper carving on
the capitals. Early English lancets have been added and a
Perpendicular east window. Some of the windows have
old glass with the arms of Neville and Scrope. There
is no chancel arch, and the chancel, narrowing towards
the east, accentuates its length; the oak roof is Tudor.
The atmosphere of the quiet country in which it stands
penetrates to the interior of this unassuming church.

John Wesley preached in the church on the morning
of 20th May 1744, and at Castle Bolton in the afternoon.
He was very pleased with the serious behaviour of both
congregations, and with the numbers at Redmire. He
came again thirty years later, this time from Swaledale,
from where he says they 'crossed over the enormous
mountain into lovely Wenandale, the largest by far of
all the Dales, as well as the most beautiful.'

Until recently wedding parties walked through the
village and up the lane to and from the church. Now
they ride in cars, and the old wedding customs have
gone. As they left the church the bridegroom threw a
handful of pennies into the beck, and the children
scrambled for them. At the end of the lane, a maid
from the Bolton Arms Hotel would be waiting with
glasses of ale on a tray. The bridal party drank their
healths, and then proceeded to the village where, at the
lane which leads to the King's Arms Hotel, the same
rite would be repeated. When they reached the house
door, the bridegroom was handed a plate piled with
pieces of wedding cake. Standing back to back with the
bride he threw this over his shoulder into the road, and

the watching crowd each picked up a piece; it was considered unlucky if the plate did not break.

At this stage, not at the church gate as was the usual custom, the bridegroom distributed 'hensilver' to the men of the village. This was spent in drinks at the inns, and a long ceremony went with it. The men sat round the inn parlour with their glasses filled, and one of them would sing this verse:

Oh, here's a good health to the bride of yond house
    That's provided us all this good cheer;
Lord send her her health,
Lord prosper her wealth,
    And may we be married next year.

Then he would pick up his glass and drink it off. It was refilled, and they all sang the second verse:

It's fair to be seen he's drunk it off clean
    As any other man can,
And if that he please
Another at his ease
    And it shall be unto a good man.

The song was sung for each man, in a tune which was almost a dirge. It was called 'singing 'em happy.'

The road past the church continues through woods to Bolton Hall and Wensley. Another lane starting near it goes to a farmhouse in the fields known as Mill House, near which is the site of a mill, mentioned in records of 1420 and 1595. Turning to the right at Mill House, the path runs down to the river. A footbridge known as the Monkey Bridge, which used to cross the river here, was washed away in a flood. Above are the

Redmire Falls, which are as lovely as the high falls at Aysgarth, but not so well known. The river flows fast below them, and overhung with trees is very beautiful.

A path turning to the east from Mill House leads to the sulphur well. About fifty years ago this well was famous all over the district, and the healing power of its waters was said to equal those of Harrogate. The spring came out of the bank just above the river, but it was broken into by the cutting of a level in the Keld Head lead mine, and ceased to flow. You can find in the grass the round stones which edged the well, and bigger stones which were part of a bath into which children and sometimes grown-ups were dipped. Floods have gradually washed them out of place. The water was drunk, and bottles of it were taken away. Paths were laid to the well, and on Sunday afternoons crowds visited it. There would be a procession of traps along the roads to Redmire; the maids from Bolton Hall would come dressed in their Sunday crinolines; and sometimes there was a band. In the morning the people would go down and bring home a bottleful to drink with their Sunday dinner. 'Wasn't it nasty?' we asked an old lady, thinking of the waters of Harrogate and Bath. 'Nasty!' she said; 'we gloried in 't!'

From time to time there has been talk of trying to recover the spring, and of making the village into a spa. Certainly the situation is there ready made, but if it had happened, Redmire's natural beauty might have gone, and there would have gone too the old-fashioned charm which it has kept through time and change.

Preston Cow Pasture

CHAPTER XVII

APEDALE AND PRESTON-UNDER-SCAR

THE road which climbs out of Redmire and goes to Grinton in Swaledale is another of the fine moorland ways which connect the two valleys of Wensleydale and Swaledale. A road turns from it to Apedale, and further along, where this meets a track to Castle Bolton, there are remains of a building called Pattinson's Houses, where miners lived.

Apedale is a desolate, forsaken valley whose life has gone with the lead mines. It has a tragic beauty. For centuries men searched and toiled there, and now it is silent. It is on the belt of lead-yielding country which runs from Nidderdale, across Wensleydale, Swaledale, and Arkengarthdale, to the moors beyond the River Tees, but it had not the depth of ore which was found in many parts; the veins suddenly became poorer and shallower. Men never quite believed this; they were always making fresh attempts to reach the ore which they felt must be there, cutting new levels and sinking shafts, though many of them lost money. There has been plenty of lead near the surface, but this was won by the early workers whom the miners speak of as 'T'owd man.'

Now the road comes to the ruins of a smelt mill and a dressing station where the lead ore was washed. Past these the eerie beauty of the valley increases. Everywhere there are signs of mines, softened and overgrown, so that what were blemishes are now part of an interesting story. To the right are great, rocky clefts in the hill. One, large enough to have a grass plot for a floor, has probably been a cave whose limestone roof was gradually worn away by water and fell in. It and most of the other clefts have been used for 'hushing,' a very early method of locating and winning ore which was near the surface; Pliny mentions it as being used in Roman times. Water was collected on the moor above, and then released, bringing down or exposing any lead ore. It was used for a long period at the upper end of Apedale. Many outlines of dams can be seen, and the hills have a scarred appearance, as though they have been swept by storms. Scattered over the moor are conical holes, the remains of shafts which have fallen in, and ruins of houses behind them show that families once lived here; near one a gooseberry bush still grows, a relic of a garden.

Only rabbit catchers, a few walkers who love its grimness, and occasionally a shepherd venture into Apedale now. But if men have left it, it is not quite alone. At each bend, dozens of rabbits scuttle to their holes, even running through the beck in their fright.

We have seen a fox emerge, glide across the grass, and disappear in a patch of bracken almost the colour of itself. Further along, a stoat slunk into a hole under some stones, where it lived, like the fox, with food close at hand.

Back on the Grinton road again, a track below the Apedale one turns east, passing a disused house, named Calamine House, probably because calamine was found near it. Mine tippings have been the means of discovering other minerals of which early diggers did not know the value, though none have been worked in large quantities.

The mines here, Cobscar Mine, Cranehow Bottom, and the Keld Head Mine, were some of the richest in the dale, and the last to be worked. Cobscar smelt mill is on the track; its chimney can be seen on the moor from a great distance. The mill is much as it was when the mining ceased; the smelting hearths remain, and it can be pictured full of activity. In another building lead moulds lie useless on the floor. Some have Lord Bolton's name on them; he owned the royalties of the mines, and received as rent a percentage of the lead, the amount varying from a sixth to a twelfth as the price of lead varied.

The moor is desolate here; it has not yet recovered from the fumes which destroyed its growth, for it received also those from the Keld Head smelt mills two miles further down in Gillfield Wood. If the fumes had been allowed to escape in the valley, they would have killed the surrounding vegetation and harmed the farms, so in the eighteenth century a chimney was built for two miles along the ground on to the moor with an out-let near Cobscar. It was one of the earliest chimneys of its kind, made by digging a ditch, covering it with an arched stone roof, and filling the crevices with turf. It is broken now in places, and the interior can be seen. When the railway first came up Wensleydale it was a favourite joke to tell the passengers to watch for the two-mile-long chimney, which they would expect to see towering into the sky. The chimney very soon paid for itself, for the fumes passing up its length solidified, and clung with the soot to the walls. At intervals the interior was scraped, and the lead thus gained was separated from the soot and smelted again.

Only a few ruins overgrown with trees remain of the Keld Head smelt mill, although it was later than the one on the moor, being built as lower levels were made in the mine, and it became inconvenient to carry the ore so far. Its stone and slates have been taken for other buildings, and the engine house lower down has suffered the same fate. As we peered into it in the dusk, a barn owl flew silently from its roofless walls.

Keld Head Mine, the largest in Wensleydale, is under this hill; its two longest levels each stretch for a mile into it, and are connected with the surface by shafts. From the lowest level, Ash Bank, to the top it is a hundred and sixty fathoms. The shafts rose in stages, so that the men, who had to climb them up vertical ladders, could rest. Flooding was the great difficulty. Expensive pumping machinery was put in, but no amount of pumping could keep it in check, and this as much as the low price of lead caused the closing of the mine.

In its best days it employed over three hundred men, between sixty and seventy men and boys being required for washing alone. In one year 1,374 tons of smelted ore were produced from it.

Most of the old miners still living worked at the Keld Head Mine; 'Keleds,' they call it, and speak of it with pride. Every detail is fresh to them. Accidents have become adventures. They remember starting out to work in the early morning in a little company, singing as they went. They began as children. Boys worked the fan which pumped good air into the levels, 'Windy King,' it was called. An old man now over eighty began work when he was nine. For about four years he earned tenpence a day; then he thought it was time he had a rise. He plucked up courage to ask the agent, who looked at him and said: 'Why, tha's nobbut a peat high,' and the boy answered: 'Tha's only a lile in theesel.' He was raised to sixteenpence. Two and sixpence a day was a regular wage for a man.

Often the men worked in partnerships of six or seven, beginners receiving eightpence where experienced men got a shilling. Sometimes a partnership would bargain for a seam of ore, receiving so much a fathom or so much a bing (eight hundredweight). At other times they would give a certain amount for the privilege of working a seam, drawing the money for the ore themselves. They remember these partnerships and just with whom they worked on certain veins. In particularly rich parts openings as big as a room were sometimes cut. An old man remembers seeing one of these when 't' lead were shinin' all round t' sides like a glass 'ouse.'

The pay varied from eight to fifty shillings a bing, and out of this the miners had to provide their own candles and gunpowder, and pay for dressing the ore. The pigs of lead were weighed in tens. Thomas Ibbetson, a weigh-man, who could not read or understand figures, always gave the correct weight by a method of arranging bits of white pot, coal, and chippings. They were paid quarterly, consequently the tradesmen had to accept their money quarterly. Pay-days are vivid to them. A group of partners sat round a board near the mine buildings, and the head man went to the office for the money, which he divided on the board, giving, say, five pounds each, then smaller sums, until it came to an end.

Those who visit the dale now perhaps rejoice that the mines with their fumes and dirt are no more, but their closing is still sufficiently near for the sadness to be remembered. The industry had graven itself on the minds and traditions of the people; it was for a time as though their life had stopped. For many it meant leaving the dale, and going to find work in the Lancashire cotton mills or the Durham coal-fields. There was about the mines a glamour which has not faded in the thoughts of the men who had anything to do with them. The work had in it much of the adventure of digging for gold. It was a gamble. You might strike a vein which was not worth the working, but you might strike a very rich one. Fortunes have been made in little time, but the men who made them usually risked them on other ventures. It was not mechanical work. The men studied the mining lore of the district in order to know which were likely to be good veins, and this developed ingenuity and alertness, the effect of which is evident in their descendants.

Limestone quarries, grinding away the face of the hill, have taken the place of the lead and coal mines on the moor. Train loads of limestone are taken from the district every day to Middlesbrough and Stockton, to be used in the making of steel.

A lane from Wensley station and the Keld Head Mine runs through a wood into Preston-under-Scar, the last of the trio of villages below this rich stretch of moor. Preston has kept more than the others the air of a mining village, and it has been slower than they in throwing off the subsequent look of decay. But nothing can rob it of its position. It lies under a rocky crag, and seems to be clinging to it. The village street ends at a gate on to the fell, and here the view of the valley and the distant hills is magnificent.

The nineteenth-century church, a chapel-of-ease to Wensley, was restored in 1934, when a reredos representing the women at the Cross was painted by Miss Muriel Metcalfe. Preston Hall lies among trees below the village; its stone-mullioned windows remain, under the plaster of one of the inner walls is a row of corbels, and a corbel head is built into one of the chimneys.

The land above the scar, known as Preston Pasture, is common land, and stretches for several miles. It is a gaited cow pasture; any one renting land in the village is allowed so many cows on it, varying from one to five, making altogether between forty and fifty. They are turned out about the middle of May and stay until the middle of September, the owners going up night and morning, and milking them in the open. Some of these are small farmers, but many have other jobs and rent smallholdings as in Bolton and Redmire. They employ a herdsman, called a 'by-law man,' to drive the cows down to the milking-place, mend the walls, and cut thistles.

The men who graze cows on the pasture form a club to which they pay an entrance fee. The club employs a 'rabbit man' to catch rabbits on the common, paying him twopence for each rabbit, or it lets the rabbit catching; and the winter grazing is let for sheep. These sums provide the wages of the 'by-law man,' and insure the cows, each of which has to be passed by the committee and marked on the horn before it is admitted to the club. If a cow dies, fifteen pounds is paid to the owner. In Preston any profits are divided amongst the members every year, but in Bolton and Redmire, which also have cow pastures, the money is left in the club, and used to buy basic slag and other manures. Just before milking time you will hear the 'by-law' man calling to his dog as he rounds up the few stray cows, but the majority, anxious to be milked, are already wending their own way down.

A stile from the cow pasture leads to the old turnpike road from Richmond to Lancaster. An opening in the woods which line the scar near the top is known as Scarth Nick, and is famous as giving the finest view of the dale. It is the great expanse which is wonderful here, with the villages settled along it, Bolton Castle conspicuous above them, and Nab End sweeping across where the valley narrows to the upper dale. Sometimes from this height you see clouds below you, and rays of light striking them curiously where the sun struggles through.

A tree near Scarth Nick used to be known as the 'Hearing Tree' because a bell was hung on it to guide travellers. Bronze Age remains which look down to those on Nab End are in a field at the summit, going back a little to the west. This is another flat terrace on the hills such as the ancient Britons chose for their dwellings. A large stone circle, perfect except at one end where it seems to disappear into the wall, was probably a village enclosure. Beyond it we discovered three dried-up dewponds, and in the heaps turned out by rabbits and moles we found flint chippings. Scarth Nick carries on the story of early life which continued on these hills to Leyburn Shawl.

Leyburn Auction Mart

CHAPTER XVIII

WENSLEY AND LEYBURN

THE roads from both sides of the valley meet in the village of Wensley. This village from which the name of the dale is taken has a softer, trimmer look than the rest. The grey cottages are there the same, and a hilly green with a fine elm tree on it, planted in 1690, but its winding roads with their stretches of clipped hedges and its air of well-being proclaim it the village of the Lord of the Manor. It looks to Bolton Hall for its existence; even the mill has been turned into a sawmill to make gates and fences for the estate. Its lack of struggle has given it serenity in place of the hardy, independent look of the upper villages. It lies nearer to the river than they do.

The entrance gates to Bolton Hall are in the middle

of the village; the hall stands back in the park. It was first built in 1678 by Charles Powlett, Marquis of Winchester, who had married the daughter of the last Lord Scrope, and later became Duke of Bolton. It took the place of the ruined castle, and it is illustrative of the greater security and the growing love of comfort that it was built on the valley, not on the hill. It contains many valuable portraits of the Scrope family, some by Van Dyck. The house was rebuilt in 1902 after being destroyed by fire.

The path running through the park to Redmire passes in about a mile Nanny Doune's well, near which is an old tree whose trunk has split into four, and which is also known as Nanny Doune's tree. There is a tradition, only faintly remembered, that Nanny Doune was a letter carrier who took letters up the dale, and that she used to sleep in this tree. She is supposed to haunt it, and the dalespeople do not like to pass it in the dark.

Wensley's chief glory is its church, one of the most beautiful and interesting in Yorkshire. It was built in the thirteenth century, but was restored and the tower rebuilt in the fifteenth century. Finial shields on the aisle buttresses, illustrating various alliances of the Scropes, prepare you for its connection with this family. The family pew of the lords of Bolton is conspicuous in the north aisle. The back and sides of this were part of a screen which Richard Lord Scrope gave to their chantry chapel in Easby Abbey near Richmond, and which at the Dissolution was removed to the site of the chantry chapel which he had founded in Wensley

church in 1399. A fifteenth-century wooden reliquary
is also said to have been brought from Easby.

The beautiful stalls in the chancel with poppy heads
and carvings of heraldic beasts were done by the Ripon
school of carvers. The church has one of the finest
brasses in England; it is fourteenth century, and represents a priest in eucharistic robes and with a chalice and
paten on the breast. It has been compared with the
brass of Abbot de la Mare in St. Albans Cathedral,
and was probably designed by the same person. A small
plate in one corner records that in 1607 Oswald Dykes,
a rector, was buried here. The brass was identified by a
note in this rector's will by which he desired to be buried
'under the stone and brass of Sir Simon de Wenselawe.'
There are wall paintings on the north, representing
'Jacob and Esau' and 'The Living and the Dead,' and
other paintings on two of the piers.

On the floor of the nave is an inscription to Richard
and John Clederow, both rectors. A custom is kept up
of resting coffins, except those of rectors, on this stone
during funeral services; and the first part of the marriage
service is performed on it. The font, dated 1662,
has the inscription: 'Church Masters looke to your
chargeis.' Carved stones dating from the ninth century
are inserted in the tower, the porch, and the north
interior wall, and a Viking sword has been found in
a burial in the churchyard.

The base and stump of a cross in the churchyard is
probably part of the old village cross, for Wensley was
once an important market town. It was granted a
market charter by Edward I in 1306. In 1563 it was

o

visited by a disastrous plague of which later parish records give the following account: '1563. The reason as some think that nothing is found written in the Register in the year of our Lord God 1563. Because that in that yeare, the visitation or plague was most hote and fearfull so y^t many fled and ye Towne of Wensley by reason of the sickness was unfrequented for a long season. As I finde By one old writeing dated 1569. By me Jo. Naylor.' Those who died from the plague were buried, not in the churchyard, but in a field called Chapel Hill. The place never recovered from this tragedy. Its market and trade eventually went to Leyburn, which developed in its stead, and Wensley sank into a quiet village. Perhaps it owes its present rather static feeling to that early disaster. Foundations of houses belonging to the bigger village are in the pastures near.

Leyburn, on the hillside a mile and a half further down the north side of the valley, was for a long period a hamlet in Wensley parish. It had a chapel-of-ease to Wensley, the foundations of which can be seen in a field called Chapel Flatts near the entrance to Leyburn Shawl.

The name Leyburn means 'stream by the clearing.' It is spelt 'Leborne' in Domesday book. At that time its dwellings were probably situated on or below the Shawl, protected by the cliff below and commanding a view of the district. After the Conquest, a village grew in the north-west corner, now called Grove Square, where the roads into it meet. When it was given its market charter this was found to be too small, and the present wide market-place came into being.

Leyburn is a pleasant place to enter. It is a typical dales town of to-day, the kind of place that could only be in the Yorkshire dales. The main street comes straight up a hill, and broadens out at the market-place, which has shops and houses on either side, and the town hall perched in the middle. It has a lighthearted, breezy air; it looks and is a healthy town. The wind comes sweeping down the street from the hills until you can scarcely stand against it. One market-day it caught a pile of bags from a stall, took them up into the air, and scattered them in all directions, like a giant snowstorm.

A market charter was granted to Leyburn in the reign of Charles II, and in 1686 the day was changed from Tuesday to Friday. A letter written from Bolton by Charles, Marquis of Winchester, to his son reads: '. . . I have also built a brigg over ye brook near John Thornton's at Riddmer which will be finisht this week y^t wee may pass thither for pleasure or business and ye countrey to Leyborne markett and faire of which last we have had 2 very great ones and ye markett is considerable and I have built 2 shambles in ye markett place and paved ye markett round about and am building a handsome tole-booth began 3 weeks since which will cost 2 or 300£ and a cross for markett women to sitt on in selling so y^t . . .' The corn market was specially paved in 1800, by which time it had become one of the biggest corn markets in the north of England. In 1844 three cheese fairs a year were originated.

Leyburn's prosperity to-day lies in its market. It has become for the lower dale what Hawes is for the upper. Like it, it has gathered in all those markets which were once held in many villages. The old market square, now a quiet corner, is used as a park on market-days. Every kind of vehicle is seen here, lorries and vans, new cars and cars whose owners have long forgotten their age, shining traps and traps devoid of varnish, and the blue wagon which comes from Bolton Hall to collect parcels. The market, chiefly for sheep and cattle, is held in the Mart to the north of the town, where, as at Hawes, the stock is sold by auction. Here again are the raised seats round the ring, and the dalespeople mingle with buyers from beyond the dale. There is the same tenseness among the groups which line the ring inside and out, half unconsciously guiding the cattle with their sticks.

Up to date as it prides itself on being, you find in the Auction Mart at Leyburn old men who look much as their grandfathers must have looked when they attended the open market, and made their slow bargains. Their weather-beaten faces are, like their clothes, not cut to a pattern. They sit on the benches with their chins resting on their sticks, living over again the days when they were young and vigorous and taking their part in it all. The auction draws them like a magnet; among the cattle and sheep, the buying and selling, they are at home.

The rest of the market is still held in the market-place. Here the women congregate at fruit and crockery and drapery stalls, and butter and eggs and Wensleydale cheeses of all sizes are sold. The men visit the tool and rope stalls at intervals in the auction; dale farms require

fewer implements and tools than lowland farms with
their arable land, and those they need grow in importance.

The cheap-jacks get their chance in the afternoon when
shopping and work are finished. There is the man who
makes cough sweets, talking incessantly as he twists
the sugary mess in his hands and stretches it like elastic.
The dalesmen wink at each other, as much as to say it
is all talk, but they are ready for the free samples.
The salesman produces a long stick of herb, and a man
calls out: 'Does it grow on t' mooer?' A woman coughs.
'Now, mother,' says the man, 'you just wait a minute,
your throat's like a razor.' 'Aye,' she retorts, 'that's
why I've come.' He does a vigorous trade with his
packets amongst the crowd. Then the buses gather,
the stall people pack up and go, and there is space and
calm again.

Leyburn Shawl is a natural terrace extending for two
miles on the rocky scar at the west end of the town, and
is famous for its view. It was laid out as a promenade
with seats and shelters in 1841, and a gala known as
Leyburn Shawl Annual Festival was held there. In
1844, the *Wensleydale Advertiser* records that this was
attended by two thousand people, 'the bulk of whom
were of the highest respectability.' It was followed by
a ball in the Bolton Arms Hotel which lasted until
four o'clock. At that time the 'Bolton Arms,' which
was the centre of the town's life, was holding morning
and afternoon concerts.

The Shawl now has a neglected appearance. The
romance has gone even from the Queen's Gap where
Mary Queen of Scots was supposed to be captured as

she tried to escape from Bolton Castle. Here again limestone is being quarried from the back of the scar; but the noise is soon left behind as you follow the path at the end through woods and fields to Keld Head. Below and beyond the Shawl there are more remains of cave dwellings and village enclosures of the Bronze Age; bones and charcoal have been found here, and a grinding stone and flints, which are preserved in Mr. Horne's museum in the market-place.

The main street looks eastwards to Bedale and the Hambleton Hills, but nearer are the little villages whose market also it is: Harmby, owned in the four-teenth century by Andrew de Harcla, who turned traitor and sided with the Scots against Edward II, and was hung, drawn, and quartered in 1323; Spennithorne with its fine church; Thornton Steward with its Norman one; and, between them, Danby Hall, the home of a branch of the Scrope family.

From Grove Square a road goes north-west over the moors to Grinton. Another, going north-east to Rich-mond, climbs through the village of Bellerby, on the moors above which grey millstone, 'used by respectable millers,' was quarried; it then crosses the roads to Down-holme and Catterick near Halfpenny House, an old toll-house, passes Hart Leap Well, and goes over open moor, to turn suddenly to the hill above Richmond, getting an unexpected view of that romantic town and castle.

This road, made in 1751, starts as a branch of the turnpike road from Richmond to Lancaster. The most direct way turned near Halfpenny House towards Scarth Nick, and kept on the north side of the valley as far as Askrigg; its toll-gates at Halfpenny House, Holly Hill, Bellerby Lane End, Ballowfield Bridge, Bainbridge, and Hawes were let by auction at the 'Bolton Arms' in Leyburn. The other way makes a curve, as traffic does to-day, to take in the town of Leyburn, the capital of the lower dale.

Wensley Bridge

CHAPTER XIX

WEST WITTON AND PENHILL

WEST WITTON, higher up on the south side of the valley from Leyburn, is reached through Wensley, crossing the River Ure there over a bridge, of which Leland says: 'The great Bridge of stone was made many yere sins by a good Person of Wencelaw caullid Alwine.' Alwine died in 1430. Built as a two-arched bridge, it was widened to double its width in the nineteenth century. The line of the old bridge can be traced under the arches, and the low parapet above.

Past a wooded stretch beside the river is the south entrance to Bolton Hall. A drive continues up the hill on the other side of the road to a small ruined building. This was built for the original Polly Peachum in Gay's *Beggar's Opera*, Lavinia Fenton, who married as his second wife the third Duke of Bolton. It is said that when she sang in the summer-house she could be heard distinctly at Bolton Hall, a mile away.

The road climbs up West Witton whose name

means 'the farm in the wood;' but there is no wood round it to-day, although it looks down to the parkland of Bolton Hall. The grey village, lying under Penhill, has a look of struggle, as if it had known poverty and a life which was not always easy. You like it better as you know more of it, for much of its reality is beneath the surface. It faces across the valley to Preston-under-Scar, with which it has much in common besides its similar position, for this also was a miner's village; it grew to its present size to house them. About fifty years ago a procession of thirty or forty men could be seen wending their way home through Bolton Park to West Witton every afternoon when the shifts in the mines had changed. Now their houses have mellowed and softened and lost their air of newness, and the village has gone back to a country place.

Many of the houses are old. One of them, Catterall Hall, was at one time so important that letters were addressed to West Witton, near Catterall. For a long period a family of the same name lived in it. The male line died out in the eighteenth century, and the house came to co-heiresses who divided it into two, pulling down a piece in the middle. The lower half is now an inn; a curious recess has been discovered in one of its walls, and it is supposed to have secret passages. Towards the end of the nineteenth century there lived in one part of it an old lady who was so poor that she lived chiefly on bread and water, and to keep warm during the night used to take three cats tied in sacks into bed with her. But every Sunday morning she went to church, wearing a dress spangled with gilt and many ribbons.

A few houses behind the main road face Penhill. An occupant of one of these was told by her neighbour who preferred her own house on the main road: 'I 'se sorry for ye livin' here, it 's a dowly spot, ye can see nowt.' But Penhill slopes back and does not overpower the village, and those who face it see its ever-changing effects. Nor is it without movement. There are still a few travellers along the road on its ridge, shepherds go over the fell, and sometimes for weeks at a time there are men on Capplebank burning waste wood after trees have been felled.

The Norman church in West Witton was pulled down and a new church built in the nineteenth century, but the sixteenth-century tower remains, and some glass in the vestry window with the arms of the abbots of Jervaulx. Until about 1780 actual burials did not take place in West Witton, because the rock was too near the surface for graves to be dug, but in that year a quantity of soil was carted to it, and the ground was consecrated and used for burials. Before that the dead were taken to Wensley, and this led to a mistaken idea that West Witton was part of Wensley parish. It was separated from Wensleydale in the twelfth century, and has since belonged neither to an abbey nor to another church. The only payment which it made was Peter's pence, threepence a year for each of the twenty houses as an Easter offering to Wensley church.

The church is dedicated to St. Bartholomew. The effigy of this saint was burnt as a winding-up to the annual feast in August, though the meaning of the custom is lost in the past. The ceremony is known as the 'Burning of Old Bartle.' The feast used to last three days, but on whatever day it fell, the 'Burning of Bartle' took place the following Saturday evening. Sports on the Saturday afternoon are all that remain of the feast, but the 'Burning of Bartle' survives. The ceremony does not begin until ten o'clock, but long before that time crowds assemble in the streets. When the inns which have been crowded all evening are closed a rowdy element creeps in. It is dark when the procession begins at the east end of the village. The two chief actors walk first, one carrying a life-size effigy of 'Old Bartle,' made of sacking stuffed with straw and with a painted face. At the last house they stop, the effigy is held up into the air, and the second man intones in a high-pitched monotonous voice:

> In Penhill Crags he tore his rags;
> At Hunter's Thorn he blew his horn;
> At Capplebank Stee he brake his knee;
> At Grisgill Beck he brake his neck;
> At Wadham's End he couldn't fend;
> At Grisgill End he made his end.

He ends with 'Shout, lads, shout' (pronounced 'shute'), at which the crowd gives a tremendous shout. They go slowly down the village, stopping at intervals to say the rhyme and shout, and collect something for the sports. The road is thronged with people, who press round 'Bartle' and the two performers.

The procession turns up Grass Gill, where the effigy is placed on a pile of wood and set on fire. Whilst 'Bartle' burns, they sing old songs, trying to make themselves heard above the crowd.

Perhaps the feast and the 'Burning of Bartle' was the

one festivity of the year in West Witton, for the village seems to have been hard-working and thrifty, and to have possessed an unusual number of craftsmen. In the seventeenth century it was famous for its wooden butter-tubs or firkins, but in 1681 a great quantity of wood which had been collected for their manufacture was burnt, and the industry never recovered. The registers show many wool-combers, and a wool-dyeing industry was carried on in the mill.

On the road about a mile west of West Witton is Swinithwaite, whose name means 'a place cleared in the forest by burning.' A branch of the Metcalfe family lived at the Hall here for many generations. Ottiwell Metcalfe and his son, of Swinithwaite, helped Sir Thomas Metcalfe in his attack on Raydale House in 1617. Their ancestor, another Ottiwell, was, in 1542, prepared to side with Christopher Metcalfe of Nappa against Lord Scrope, 'because he was the head of his kin.' The tiny hamlet beyond it seems to shrink back from the road.

Temple Farm, a little further to the west, has the following inscription over one of its doorways:

> Whoso shall com
> into this hous O L
> ord Do them prote
> ct and who doth p
> as forth of the sam
> e Jesv there waye de
> rect. P. AIMA. 1608.

The farm gets its name from a Knights Templars' chapel on the hill above. Built into the wall on the south side of the road, between it and Swinithwaite Hall, is a stone about sixteen inches square, incised with a double cross; the ancient badge of the order before it was established in England in 1146.

The path to the Templars' chapel is beyond the farm, up a field, at the top of which it turns to the left through a wood. It is nearly a hundred years since a Mr. Anderson, then living at Swinithwaite Hall, excavated a curious mound on the hill, and discovered the foundations of this chapel and other buildings, some spurs, horse-bits, and fragments of ancient armour. The walls of the chapel are a yard thick, and are left for about two feet above ground; there is an opening for the south door, and bases of pillars and the worn step are still in place. In the interior are the steps to the sanctuary, the base of the altar, a stone piscina and two small stone coffins. Larger coffins, now outside the walls, held skeletons when they were discovered.

The site was given to the Templars soon after 1146 by the family of Akar who founded Fors Abbey. Land was acquired later in many parts of Wensleydale, extending as far north as Lunds. A grant of land was made in the early thirteenth century to 'maintain a light perpetually burning in the chapel of Penhil.' The chapel was dedicated to God, the Virgin, and St. Catherine, the patron saint of the linen weavers, and an important personage to the Templars, whose garments were largely of linen.

The Templars gave shelter to travellers in their hospice here, called Temple Dowskar, a name which was eventually used to describe all their territory in the dale. The brotherhood in Wensleydale suffered severely in the inquiries made against the Knights Templars. John de Bellerby, Master of the House of Penhill, was one of twenty locked up in York Castle to await trial in 1309.

A path leads from the chapel to a road which runs along the slope of Penhill to Middleham Moor, the road which starts at the pack-horse bridge in West Burton. It has been considered to be the Roman road from Middleham to Bainbridge, and was for long used as a short way from Aysgarth and West Burton. From the first rise you can see West Burton at the foot of Waldendale. No roads are visible from here, and the place has a forsaken look, and appears like a crude drawing of an earlier village. Going eastwards, the sweeping hills near West Witton seem to dwarf the valley. Drovers brought their cattle this way to Middleham Moor Fair; on the day before the fair, West Witton people saw a continual procession moving slowly along the ridge.

At the corner where Grass Gill Lane turns down to West Witton there is an eighteenth-century milestone, a square pedestal, with the names, Hawes, Askrigg, Middleham, and Carlton on the sides. It shows the directions of the old roads over the hills, leading from one dale to another convenient for pack-men and drovers. At Stoups Stob, just before Capplebank, the road forks, and goes separate ways into Coverdale, and so to Middleham. From the higher road a track turns up to Penhill Beacon.

Penhill, dividing Waldendale and Coverdale, and rearing its domed summit as a barrier in Wensleydale, is the best known of all the dale hills. It and Waldendale are isolated examples of the survival of early British names in Wensleydale; 'pen' comes from a word which means 'head.' It looks out on to its three dales in a paternal manner.

Penhill Beacon, 1,685 feet, is the Wensleydale end of the hill. It was chosen in olden days for the lighting of beacons, forming one of a chain which went round England. Here, on the 6th May 1935, a beacon was lit to celebrate the Silver Jubilee of the reign of King George V and Queen Mary.

Either way nothing hides the view. There are the trees among which Jervaulx Abbey lies, Middleham church tower peeps over the ridge, pointing the way to new sights, and Leyburn perches on the hill across; you can trace the dale through Castle Bolton, Askrigg, and Hawes into these hill regions which you know and love; and you see too how the parkland and the meadows bordered by hedges give place to walls and scanty trees, and they in their turn to these rocky slopes.

The summit of Penhill lies beyond the Beacon. The way is not so easy here; there is no track along the top, and the surface is boggy. After the Beacon it seems remote and forgotten, although in places you can look down on to the green meadows of Bishopdale. A little beyond the summit is the track from Cote Farm in Waldendale to Carlton in Coverdale. A more adventurous way to Carlton is to follow the Old Peat Road. When all the farmers dug and gathered peat this was a well-kept track; now in places it is a cart track, showing the ruts made by wheels, and in others it loses itself in the moor. It runs down, at first through thick bracken, into a lane which ends at Carlton, entering at one corner of that mile-long village, the largest place in Coverdale.

Horse House, Coverdale

CHAPTER XX

COVERDALE

COVERDALE is one of Wensleydale's alien children, a wayward valley, amazing to find so near the foot of the dale. It must be sought; there is no suggestion as you take the roads to it of this valley at the end. Four roads lead to it from Wensleydale, from West Witton, Middleham, and East Witton, but all go over open common, before dropping down into Coverdale.

It is a miniature of the larger dale with its own abbey, villages, and hills. In its twelve miles it passes from the wooded softness around Coverham Abbey to the solemn hills which shut it in at the head, isolating and guarding it against change. A mountain pass leads out of it to

Wharfedale over the lower slopes of Great Whernside. The road up the valley was once the coach route from London to Richmond, coming via Barnsley, Halifax, Skipton, and Kettlewell to Coverhead and Middleham. The way through is now only used by walkers and cyclists and more daring motorists. The few passing cars are regarded as an interest, not a nuisance. We remember how, as we went through Carlton one Saturday evening in summer, the people sitting outside their doors waved to us, friendly waves which had in them the joyous feelings of a Saturday night, and a Sunday's holiday to come.

Coverdale is the largest of the dales which run into Wensleydale, large enough to support a life of its own. That and its position have kept its people simple and unspoilt. Many of the genuine dalespeople whom you see in Leyburn on market-days have come from Coverdale, and the old-fashioned traps have brought them. Its seclusion has resulted in much intermarrying, and it is not to be wondered at that superstition has kept a hold here, that old customs and beliefs which have their origin in pagan days survive. The ghost of a black dog comes with important events and decisions, and as a warning of death. Sometimes it is headless, sometimes described as having eyes like 'pewter doublers' (dishes). It appears to any one who walks backwards round a particular barn seven times, making a wish. If the dog turns its back on them they will die within the year, but if it puts its front paws on to their shoulders they will get their wish. The thorn tree is still held in awe as sacred. Not many years ago a Coverdale man who lived

P

far from a church used to take his family to say their prayers under a thorn tree every Sunday morning.

The village of Carlton, resting under Penhill, is the centre of the dale, though it has lost the importance it possessed when Coverdale was a forest, and the courts of the forest were held in the Hall Cote. This is mentioned in the Middleham accounts of 1465–7, and they also mention a common oven and brewery and a water corn mill. It is thought that an ancient parliament was held on the large mound with an elm on the top in the centre of the village. The name Carlton means 'Karl's farm,' but it is now a place of small farms. The houses line the main street. Some have the dignity of age, proof of which lies in their inscribed doorways. You pick one out here and there on its long length; the old Hall, now a farmhouse, has the date 1659 in raised letters. A house with an inscription on a large stone was the home in the nineteenth century of Mr. Henry Constantine, a writer of dialect prose.

As we arrived in Carlton one hot day in summer, a blue car stopped at the roadside, and two women stepped out of it. They were dressed alike, in navy-blue dresses, felt hats, black boots, and woollen stockings, and had an air of the sea about them. Then we saw that the back of the car had been turned into a table for fish. The women went from house to house selling it in a business-like manner, and seemed something very much of the present brought into this out-of-the-way dale.

Roads and paths start out in all directions from Carlton, across the valley, to the hamlet of Melmerby, and up Penhill. Above Carlton the main road climbs up the valley. Villages and houses by their names tell the tale of the forest: Gammersgill, 'Gamel's hut,' Swineside, 'swine pasture,' Hindlethwaite, 'forest clearing for hinds,' Arkleside, 'Arkel's pasture,' Bradley, 'broad clearing,' Hunter's Hall. The many cultivation ridges on the sides of the hills show the age of these settlements.

At Gammersgill, a hamlet of farmhouses, there seem to be more cows than at any place in the dale. You see them grazing in the fields, and rubbing and jostling each other in the roads at milking time as they pass from the pastures to the barns.

Horse House, the next village, through which the coaches from London to Richmond passed, is said to have received its name from the fact that pack-horses were rested and fed here; its name may have been gradually altered at that time from an earlier and similar form. There is now one inn, but in those busier days there were two. A house high above the road was the other; it has a long stone porch at the back of it where the men placed their food, and a hole in the garden, now partly filled in, was the dog pit where drovers' dogs were put for the night.

One evening in haytime a group of men came out of the inn at Horse House, among them two Irishmen who started to quarrel. It was an unusual scene for the dales: the farmers and farm men leaning against the inn wall in the dusk, looking stolidly on, whilst the Irishmen stood gesticulating and arguing in their rich, excitable voices, making drama of their quarrel. It was very different from the quarrels and feuds of the dalespeople, in which a dogged obstinacy seems to prevail. Starting from a trivial cause, these often last through generations, growing in bitterness.

The little church in the midst with its rough stone walls fits into the picture. In 1607 Thomas Jenkinson, a curate here, was indicted in the Quarter Sessions Record for allowing piping and other disorders in the chapel on St. Simon's Day. At the same time Anthony Yeoman was charged with harbouring rogues.

Beyond it the road grows narrower, shut in on either side by banks with a wall and often a hedge as well on the top. Passing the hamlets of Bradley and Woodale, it swings out on to the moor, and starts its slow climb. Hunter's Hall, now a farmhouse, is on the site of an old hunting hall of the Lords of Middleham. On the summit, just before the road dips down to Wharfedale, there is an ancient entrenchment.

Another road which turns up the fells at Arkleside below Bradley was a pack-horse road to Nidderdale. Packmen used it on their way from Scotland to the West Riding towns, coming through Kirkby Stephen, and down Wensleydale. You can imagine the horses bending their heads as they took this hill, passing slowly a row of boundary stones, until they breasted the summit, and saw before them the valley of Nidderdale to which they were going. To-day the two great reservoirs of the Bradford Corporation, Angram and Scar Head, have made the head of this valley into lakes, but the packmen would see only the beginnings of the River Nidd, a hamlet, and a few farmhouses.

The packmen were in the habit of putting up at a

little inn kept by a woman and her daughter at Lodge, on the Nidderdale side of the moor. Coming as they did year after year, these packmen were well known, and it began to be noticed that several of them ceased to come. After about two years their wives travelled down from Scotland to look for their husbands. Inquiries proved that the missing men had always been seen last either at Horse House in Coverdale or Middlesmoor in Nidderdale. It was noticed too that the people at the inn seemed prosperous, and that many of the farmers in the district were using Scotch ponies and their wives wearing Paisley shawls. A search was made, and the bodies of the victims, all headless, were found buried near the house. There is an entry in the books of the township of Middlesmoor for the 30th May 1728: 'Three murder'd Bodies were found burrd on Lodge End without heads,' but there is no record of the end of the story which says that the woman and her daughter were tried and hanged.

Whether from this happening or not, the hill over which the road goes is now called 'Dead Man's Hill.' It is a peaceful place, silent but for walkers and shepherds, and on the few occasions when shooters lunch in the hut on the summit. Contemplating this scene of murders you realize how easy it was, but you wonder at the strangeness of human beings who, with the moors and wind and expanse of sky around them, should plan such deeds for worldly possessions of little use here.

At Arkleside a path runs along the south side of the River Cover, passing Hindlethwaite Hall, an ancient manor house, goes through the hamlet of Swineside on a ridge of the hill, and joins the road at West Scrafton, the largest village on this side of the valley.

The name Scrafton means 'the town by a hollow in the earth,' and fits the village well, for hills rise sheerly above it, gaunt and forbidding, after the manner of Welsh mountains. It appears to be wrapped up in itself. An old woman in a sun-bonnet resting on the green after a day in the hay-fields added to the vivid impression which the village gave.

Next comes East Scrafton, where the Methodists had a bad reception. They held a meeting in an inn, and as the minister gave out the hymn, *Vain, delusive world, adieu*, the floor gave way, and the congregation found themselves in the cellar below. The roof beam had been nearly sawn in two.

An ancient lane with holly trees meeting above it leads to the river and the ruins of St. Simon's chapel. This was built for the convenience of the people of the upper dale in winter, and a hermit, appointed by the monks of Coverham Abbey, lived at one end of it, and used to clean it. He was given all the offerings made to St. Simon, and these would probably be considerable, for a ford crossed the river here. The chapel does not seem to have been used after the Dissolution, for in 1582 it was called 'a ruined chapel.' In 1586 a John Prat was keeping an alehouse in it. There is said to have been a stone in the wall which read: 'Yf ye require or ye desire to wete who built this place. Sir Randall Pigott.'

The ruins of the chapel, which seems to have been little more than a barn, are overgrown, and ash saplings spring from the midst of them. The site, with wooded scars behind it and a steep bank on the opposite side, has a shut-away feeling. Only the paths which run up from the ford tell of the outside world and traffic which has long since ceased. Tits and golden-crested wrens, their chirruping like the tinkle of an old musical box, flutter in the top branches of the ashes and sycamores beside the river. You can picture the hermit living there, like St. Francis, with the birds for company as he tended the chapel.

Steps like those of an ancient causeway lead up the scar from the ruins, and a path with a wicket at the end comes out at the road. Now a beck is crossed by a new concrete bridge, and just behind it is Ulla Bridge, which it replaced. The road curved to cross Ulla Bridge, for its builders placed it where the beck was narrowest. You can see under the arch how it was first made only half the width for pack-horse traffic. Its stones, green with moss, seem to have taken on the colour of the hills and trees, and it fits unassumingly into the scene, carrying you back in spirit to the times for which it was built.

Passing Caldbergh the road runs swiftly down, drawing ever nearer to the river, until at Coverham it meets the road which connects it with the other side of the valley. Itself it goes straight on, passing Braithwaite Hall, a seventeenth - century manor house which has its original oak panelling in the hall and an upstairs room. This is now a farm, and long stacks of bracken round it show one of the harvests of the hills which are always near in Coverdale. The road beyond it narrows into a lane on its way to East Witton.

The road to Coverham Abbey crosses the River Cover over a bridge with an unusual double arch, probably the bridge which Leland mentions as being 'a very little above the Priorye.' You can picture the gentle monks passing over it as a modern poet of Middleham does when he writes:

> The old bridge dreams that its echoes greet
> Panniered mules and sandalled feet.

The Cover here, as all down its course, is a beautiful river, never silent on its rocky bed.

Much of the charm of the abbey to-day lies in its surroundings. Few walls are left, and these are enclosed in houses or gardens, and cannot be seen as a whole. But there is the air of peace and contentment which abbey sites never seem to lose, and it is easy to imagine the white-robed monks of this Premonstratensian Order going about their work here and holding their services. There was 'good singing at Coverham.'

Coverham Abbey, like Jervaulx, was not built at first on its present site. It was founded some time before 1189 by Helewisia, wife of Robert FitzRalph, the builder of Middleham Castle keep, at Swainby, near Pickhill, on the River Swale. Helewisia died in 1195, and was buried at Swainby. In 1212, owing to many disputes with the canons, her son, Ranulph FitzRobert, removed the house to Coverham where he could more easily assert his authority. His mother's body was brought to the new abbey, and reburied in the chapter-house.

The ruins are reached along a lane below the bridge, under the arch of the inner gatehouse, built about 1500.

A house on the right is built on to the remains of the guest house which originally formed the west wall of the cloisters; it has early sixteenth-century windows, and a contemporary doorway with an inscription. Most of the remains of the church are in the garden behind and not open to visitors, but the west aisle doorway can be seen, and through it two clustered piers of the south arcade and part of the west wall of the north transept.

The farmhouse to the south has been completely built from the stones of the abbey; carved stones are dotted amongst the rest, and a carved slab similar to that at Bear Park is built into one of the outhouses. Two weathered thirteenth-century stone figures in chain armour near it represent Ranulph FitzRobert, the son of the founder, and his son, Ralph FitzRanulph. There are floriated grave slabs and several stone coffins in the farmyard which is on the site of the chancel. But these are all jumbled pieces, confusing to the mind, and you turn from them again to the harmony of the site.

The dissolution of the monastery brought poverty and hardship to the dale. It had employed women for the washing, and twenty-four male servants in the bakehouse, brewery, kitchens, and fishponds, and it had been a resting-place for travellers from Yorkshire into Lancashire. The mill below the church was first built by the monks who may also have built the mill race above it, for this is made in a primitive fashion from large slabs of stone hollowed out to make a channel.

The church on the hill behind was built in the thirteenth century in the time of the abbey. It wears a pathetic air, as if in its early days it was overpowered by the importance of the abbey church, and yet has lost something of itself with its going. It was an ailseless church, but a Decorated aisle and a Perpendicular tower have been added. It is possible to stand in a corner of its hilly graveyard, and neither see the church nor hear the bells when they are ringing. Miles Coverdale, the translator of the Bible, is thought to have been born at Coverham.

The road by the church runs down the north side of the valley to Middleham. Presently it passes Rowntree's cheese dairy, which has long been a feature of Coverdale, and goes past Cotescue Park over Middleham Low Moor. The lower end of Coverdale shares in the industry of horse breeding and training for which Middleham is famous, an industry which seems far removed from the wild upper part of the dale with its lingering superstitions.

Middleham Castle

CHAPTER XXI

MIDDLEHAM

THE sense of expectancy with which you approach Middleham changes to one of satisfaction on entering it. You are conscious that if it had not been here like this you would have been disappointed; without it much of the interest of what has gone before would fade. With its ancient castle and church, and its recollection of past glory, it is a perfect culmination to the dale. From either end of Wensleydale you reach it up a hill, and the castle stands as a romantic background to the town, but from the Coverdale road you pass the castle walls to come down to the cobbled market-place. The houses are ranged chiefly round two squares, after the plan of a Breton town. In each of these is a market cross, and the church lies just beyond. The memory hangs over it of the great people of England, kings and queens and barons, who have lived within its castle walls and made it what it is.

Middleham Castle was built for residence rather than defence. When Robert FitzRandolph started it in 1170, the country was settling down after the Conquest. He built the keep, and a rough curtain wall which was pulled down and rebuilt in the thirteenth century. In 1270, Ralph FitzRanulph dying without a male heir, the castle came, through the marriage of his daughter Mary, to the Neville family; her son, Ralph, was the first Lord Neville. From this time its story is the story of the rise and fall of this important family. Many of the Nevilles were great men, but they reached their zenith in Richard, Earl of Warwick, known as 'The Kingmaker.' In the days of his power Middleham came to be known as 'The Windsor of the North.' Warwick lived in regal state here; old papers tell of the lavish meals for his many retainers; 'six oxen were eaten at breakfast, and every tavern was full of his meat, for who that had any acquaintance in that house he should have so much sodden and roast as he might carry upon a long dagger.' Edward IV stayed here while Warwick was on the Yorkist side, and later was made a prisoner in the castle.

After Warwick, the last of the great feudal barons, was killed at Barnet in 1471, Middleham was forfeited to the Crown. Edward IV gave it to his brother, Richard, Duke of Gloucester, afterwards Richard III, who had married Warwick's daughter. Here Richard's only son was born, and died suddenly in 1484 when he was eight years old. After the death of Richard III at Bosworth the splendour of Middleham declined. In 1646 the Parliamentary committee ordered it to be rendered untenable, and for two and a half centuries it became a quarry of ready dressed stone from which most of the Middleham of to-day was built.

A drawbridge led to the entrance, which is under the north-east tower, through a vaulted arch with a guard chamber on the east side. The Norman keep in the centre is the fourth largest in England. In it were the Great Hall, with an open hearth in the middle, the sleeping compartments, and the Chamber of Presence. Circular stairs led from it to the battlements, and to the vaulted kitchens and cellars, where there was a well. At the east end is a thirteenth-century chapel which had two stories below it. Doorways south of the Hall led to wooden bridges which stretched over the court to the rooms in the curtain wall.

A round tower at the south-west corner is called the Prince's Tower from a tradition that Prince Edward was born in it. The nurseries in the west curtain led from it, and under them was the bakehouse, in which there are traces of three ovens. The brewhouse, which has a horse mill, was in the south curtain.

This style of castle is a step towards those in which the buildings ran round a small courtyard as at Bolton. In this stage of its development the nearness of the curtain walls to the keep must have made the inner rooms gloomy and airless. Most of the dressed stone has gone from the lower parts; in places so much has been taken that it is surprising how the walls stand. But you can climb almost to the top of the keep, and see the hills shutting in the dale, and see too how birds nest and call about the walls within which kings and princes feasted.

The castle had a very different appearance in the middle of the nineteenth century before ruins were valued. Important visitors to the town were then not allowed to see it because of the slovenly interior littered with unsightly objects. There was a blacksmith's shop in one tower, and a cartwright's in the other. A gang of sweeps lived in it, and there were saw-pits and sheds, and kennels for a pack of hounds. On one of the towers a man had made a garden where he grew vegetables; he even tried gooseberries, but he gave these up because boys climbed the ruins and stole them.

Foundations of a Roman villa and remains of a hypocaust have been discovered in a field east of the castle. Behind the castle is William's Hill, the site of the first Norman building, a motte and bailey castle which was probably occupied for a hundred years. There is again the tradition here that any one who runs three times round William's Hill will find an opening in the earth which will admit him to wondrous treasure, but the feat has not yet been accomplished.

From the summit you look down on to the stately grey walls of the castle which replaced the primitive one here. On a branch of a tree beside you there hangs a dead rook, its black wings and feathers shot with a rich blue, its grim fate telling which are the chief marauders on William's Hill to-day.

A row of cottages looking across the road on to the front of the castle stand on the ground where the outer baileys would be. The castle seems to like it so, to take pleasure in the company of these now that it is deprived of nobles and kings. A cottage opposite the entrance used to be a bakehouse. It had a beehive oven in the garden where, fifty or sixty years ago, an old couple named Yeoman baked brown bread and sold it in the district.

Narrow roads lead down the hill, and on either side are cottages clinging together in that manner which only houses clustering round a castle seem to achieve; as though, long after the need for it was past, they sought its protection, even those built after its walls ceased to have the power to help or harm. The vandalism which stripped the walls of castles and abbeys and took the stone for building was strong here, destroying more than the soldiers did. But if its destruction had to be, it is good to think that the town keeps within itself the stones of the castle whose coming first made it into a town.

In the upper market is the old Swine cross, standing on a platform with steps on two sides. It consists of two stone blocks, on one of which is a mutilated figure of a beast representing either the bear of the house of Warwick or the silver boar of Richard III, the patron of the market. Near it is the bull ring. The market charter for Middleham was granted by Richard II to his cousin, Ralph Neville, in 1388; it allowed a weekly market and an annual fair. In 1479 Richard, Duke of Gloucester, obtained a Court of Piepowder to try immediately offences connected with the fair or market.

The fair was held first on the 25th October, and later on the 5th and 6th November. It became the largest cattle fair in the north of England, famous as Middleham Moor Fair. Sheep were sold the first day, and cattle and horses the second. The house doors were barricaded against cattle, so great were the numbers brought through the town; and unbroken colts and ponies galloped wildly up and down the streets. Two wooden huts were put up for bankers, and every innkeeper in the neighbourhood had a booth. The plaids of the Scottish drovers, and the bright scarves and ribbons of the gipsies, made splashes of colour in what must often have been grey November days. Like other fairs, Middleham declined in importance, and it is now merged in the Autumn Mart at Leyburn, which, if not so picturesque, is more comfortable for buyers and sellers.

The 5th November, the date of the fair, is St. Alkelda's Day. The church is dedicated to St. Alkelda, the Saxon martyr who is said to have been strangled by two Danish women. The glass in the west window of the north aisle represents her martyrdom. During restorations in 1878 female bones were discovered under the floor in the north aisle where the saint had always been said to be buried. A field's length from the west end of the church, near the path, is a well known as 'St. Alkelda's Well,' which has always been considered to have healing powers. Any one who passes may drink from it. In 1640 the people of Middleham were summoned 'for not repairing their several streets leading from Middleham Moor to the Eastern boundary of the vill and from the Market-place at Middleham to St. Awkell's Well.' This seems to suggest that a road then passed the well.

The church is mainly fourteenth century, but zigzag carving on the north exterior and thirteenth - century jambs to the south doorway indicate an earlier building. The Perpendicular tower was built for defence; it has a fireplace made from old tombstones, one of which, incised with a cross and keys, was probably that of a constable of the castle. The church was built when the Nevilles and their castle were at the height of their glory. It has a look of expectancy, as if it still wondered why all the pomp and ceremony had ceased.

In 1479 Richard, Duke of Gloucester, made Middleham church collegiate, with a dean, six chaplains, four clerks, and six choristers. He intended to build a house for the canons, but died before he had accomplished it, and the church never became fully collegiate. Henry VII took away the college land, but its privileges were revived in the reign of Charles II. In 1845 the collegiate foundation was suppressed by Act of Parliament. Charles Kingsley was the last canon to be appointed; on one of his visits he wrote to his wife of the lovely scenery round the River Cover. A memorial window to Richard III was placed in the south aisle of the church in 1934 by the 'White Boar Society,' though not every one agreed in thus honouring Richard. The glass is in late fifteenth - century style, and has figures of Richard III, his queen, and their son.

A curious gallery erected in 1804 over the north aisle is still in place; it has four box pews. A sepulchral slab with mitre and pastoral staff and the rebus of Abbot Thornton of Jervaulx who died in 1533 probably came from the abbey.

In October 1607 there was convicted at Richmond

Q

one 'Chas. Parishe of Midleham, Parish Clerke, for receiving divers persons into his dwelling-house during the time of Divine Service, and permitting them to play at unlawful games, vis: Shovell a board, etc., and also for an assault in the parish church of Midleham on one Brian Sweeting.'

The town was the centre of the forest government of Wensleydale. The last forest eyre for all the Richmond-shire forest of which there is any record was held at Middleham on the 12th August 1539 when John, Lord Scrope, was Warden of the Forest. Foresters and bow-bearers attended from 'Bishopdale, Coverdale, Waldale, Radale, and Bardale.' It records that William Connyers Esq., bow - bearer of the New Forest, re - ceived 40s., a stag in summer, a hind in winter, and all the 'blowen woode.' In the surrounding country there were a number of parks, of which Sunskew, and Cotescue in Coverdale, whose names are still in use, were two. Deer were driven into the parks and kept there.

The life of the forest, the market, and the castle has gone, but Middleham has kept alive and developed its ancient industry of breeding and training race-horses. The monks of Jervaulx Abbey first bred horses in this district, finding pasture to suit them and moors on which to exercise them. A letter written in the year 1537 says: '. . . I think that at Jervaulx and in the granges incident with the help of their great large commons, the king's highnes by good overseers should have there the most best pasture that should be in England, hard and sound of kind. For assuredly the breed of Jervaulx for horses was the tried breed of the north; the stallions and mares so well sorted that I think in no realm should we find the like to them, for there is high and large grounds for the summer, and low grounds to serve them.' To-day Middleham has some of the principal racing establishments in the country, and many noted winners and jockeys have been trained here. Everywhere you see the stable men and boys in their neat breeches. Horses are exercised on Middleham Moor, where lines are laid for running and branches and heather piled for jumping.

The pasturage rights on the moor are owned in the summer by gait-owners, and in the winter by the commoners, householders resident in Middleham. The commoners now let their rights to the horse trainers; the rent received goes to improvements in the town, and in addition each householder gets ten shillings a year. Part of the moor used to be known as Old Penhill Park.

So the links of Middleham's one large industry go far into the past; it is not a new feature which has crept in to change it. It is the old for which Middleham stands. It seems to connect and make into a whole all the ancient places of the dale, those we have seen, and the abbey which is to come. Its grandeur and dignity enhance their dignity, and in no way belittle them. It has the medieval quality of keeping to itself, and resenting interference from outside; like the men of the Middle Ages, the inhabitants take a personal interest in the government of their town—council meetings are crowded. It does not take easily to new people and new ideas. Wrapped round with old traditions, its pride and independence have kept the town individual, and the result is fascinating.

Q2

East Witton

CHAPTER XXII

EAST WITTON AND JERVAULX ABBEY

THE dale begins to open out below Middleham. The hills slope away to the north, but Witton Fell is still a barrier on the south. And Jervaulx Abbey is as yet only a tale.

The road to East Witton crosses the River Cover at Cover Bridge, built in the eighteenth century to replace an earlier one. The bridge and the inn below it make a group worthy of connecting the castle and the abbey. From here looking to the north you can see Ulshaw Bridge, the beautiful bridge which crosses the Ure, for the two rivers are drawing close.

The Ure and the Cover meet almost unnoticeably; islands in the river-bed help to disguise it, and the channel becomes very little wider. The river here is haunted by the Kelpie or Waterhorse. He comes only a few times in the year, when he rises like a white wraith from the water, and rushes over the meadows eager for prey, his object being to frighten his victims into the river. If you see nothing in the Kelpie but mist rising from the river, you will escape much terror, but then you will never know the thrill of having eluded him.

This is a famous part for fishing, and the Cover Bridge Inn is well known by fishermen. Until a few years ago the inn had been kept for centuries by members of the Towler family, who possessed the recipe for Wensleydale cheese which was used by the monks of Jervaulx, who are said to have given it to the innkeeper at Cover Bridge at the Dissolution. The cheese was first known as Coverham cheese.

Then the road comes to East Witton, resting under Witton Fell. Most of the village is off the main road, and the houses lie in a neat but not too even line up both sides of a green decorated by trees. It has a look of unreality as you pass through, but following the road round the green you find it substantial enough. This was probably the original plan of the village, but the actual houses are not old, having been rebuilt at the beginning of the nineteenth century. At the top corner the road slips quietly away into Coverdale.

The village well at the bottom of the green has its tap fixed into a very large glacial boulder; this was brought from a field a quarter of a mile away where it had been carried by glaciers during the Ice Age. It weighs over three tons, and sixteen horses were needed to get it to its present position. There are two more taps further up the green, for very few of the houses have water laid into them.

East Witton is another of those places which lost their

early importance because of the plague; in 1563 this was so terrible that it was ordered that the market be moved to Ulshaw Bridge, and the village never recovered it. The charter for it had been granted to the monks of Jervaulx, who possessed a corn mill and a fulling mill at East Witton at the time of the Dissolution.

The church was built in 1809 by the Earl of Ailesbury, to commemorate the fiftieth year of the reign of George III. The old church, which was pulled down and its stone used in the new building and the new houses, was in the tiny hamlet of Lowthorpe which joins East Witton at the south-east. It was a Norman church, and belonged to the abbey. No stone of it is left; instead, sycamores rise in this peaceful corner, where once the nave and chancel stood. The churchyard remains, and is still used as a burial ground. Many of the graves have brass plates, and some record the deaths of braziers. There is a tradition that in Catholic days it was the custom to carry the coffin once round the churchyard, sprinkling it with holy water from a stone bowl which stood on the east side.

East Witton owes much of its beauty to its background of Witton Fell, whose cliff-like end rounds off the dale. You recognize Witton Fell from a long distance by the line of larch and pine trees waving on its summit, for it differs in that from the higher fells. The trees here and on the lower slopes enrich the changing picture of the fell, adding to its normal colouring of bracken, grass, and heather, the dark green of pines, the delicate new green of larch trees, and the red, almost autumnal colouring of budding oaks.

A walk up the fell goes past the graveyard and the
few farms at Lowthorpe to a gamekeeper's cottage.
Here, turning through a gate into the woods, you can
follow a crumbling path and a bridge across the beck
to a waterfall. Dippers haunt this fall in the wood,
skimming up its surface, and preening themselves as they
perch on the rock.

The track continues above the gamekeeper's, going
between plantations where you smell the fresh scent of
pine, and see beyond the green undergrowth at the
edges a dark carpet of pine needles. A farmhouse on
the left has the enticing name of Thirsting Castle. Then
it is open fell again; rabbits stamp and disappear at
your coming, and curlews call above. The path drops
to Sowden Beck House, a hidden farm where we found
an old man chopping wood.

'What o'clock is 't?' he asked us.

We told him, then asked him the way to the Cast-
a-Way Well. He looked puzzled for a moment, then
he smiled. 'Oh,' he said, 'ye mean Slaverin' Sal.
I should hardlies do it to-night, it's too far.' We
decided that a well with such a name needed time to
be explored.

'Slaverin' Sal,' the local name for the Cast-a-Way or
Diana's Well, is on the higher slopes of Witton Fell.
It is reached by a lane starting at the south end of the
village and passing Tilsey Folly, a building, now a barn,
with a large window and carved stones which have
evidently come from the church or abbey. A track
turning to the right along a ridge leads to the well.

You soon see why the well is called 'Slaverin' Sal,'

for what appears to be the grotesque face of a Norman corbel has been used for the spout, the water coming from the mouth. Beside the well is a stone shelter lined with wood, and with a large slab of rock for a table. It was erected by the same Earl of Ailesbury, who made a carriage road to it from his house at Jervaulx, two miles to the east. This started between an avenue of trees, and came up through the wood past the gamekeeper's cottage. The family and guests at Jervaulx used to come in carriages to the well for picnics. It all seems part of an age of leisure when pleasures had to be found close at hand, and when those pleasures were dallied over. They must have been like the picnics and drives in the novels of Jane Austen. The stone table would be spread with the same elaborate meals, and probably the water from 'Slaverin' Sal' was used for their tea. You seem to slide into that atmosphere as you sit in the grotto, to hear the impatient stamp of the horses' feet, ready for home.

Pins and other articles used to be thrown into the well for luck. A rhyme about East Witton says:

Whoever eats Hammer nuts, and drinks Diana's water,
Will never leave Witton town while he's a rag or tatter.

Hammer Wood, near by, is famous for its nuts.

Here at the well you get a last view from a height in Wensleydale. Ploughed fields show here and there, dark against the green, for the valley is opening out to another life from that of the dale. To the west the upper dale is softened in the evening light as you bid it farewell.

Jervaulx Abbey is two miles further down the valley

on the road to Masham and Ripon. The site, reached
by the monks after so much trouble and disappointment,
is a beautiful one, shut in at the east, and looking up
the dale. The abbey prospered and grew here from the
beginning. The monks farmed, made cheese and bred
horses, and kept their granges up and down the valley;
smelted iron and lead; worked corn and woollen mills;
and for over three hundred years were the biggest influence in the dale. Little of the abbey remains; in
some ways it is a disappointing ruin. But its story seems
to haunt each stone, and the shady hollow has an air
of remembrance.

The stones were taken as they were taken from Middleham Castle—you find them in unexpected places, trefoiled
windows and fragments of carving—until by 1805 there
was so little left that the ground had to be excavated
to find the foundations of the church. This is now laid
with red gravel, and is easy to distinguish. The church
was one of the earliest buildings, being late twelfth
and early thirteenth century. The nave had ten bays,
the two east ones forming the monks' choir and the
the west ones the choir of the lay brothers. The base
of some of the piers remain, and the altar base and a
curious floor piscina in one of the south bays. Down the
centre of the nave are grave slabs with incised crosses
fleury and inscriptions.

The monks entered for the night services by a staircase into the south transept. The lay brothers entered
their choir by a beautiful twelfth - century, circular -
headed door on the south-west. This was also the doorway by which the monks re-entered the church after

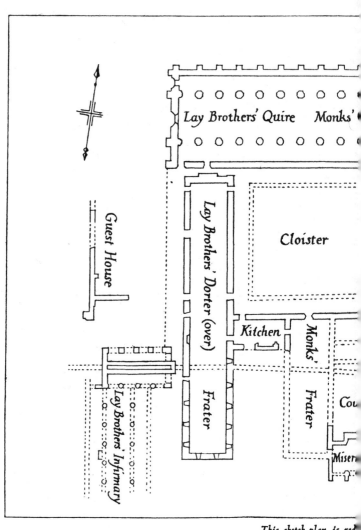

Lay Brothers' Quire   Monks'

Cloister

Guest House

Lay Brothers' Dorter (over)

Kitchen

Monks'

Frater

Frater

Cou

Lay Brothers' Infirmary

Miser

This sketch-plan is red

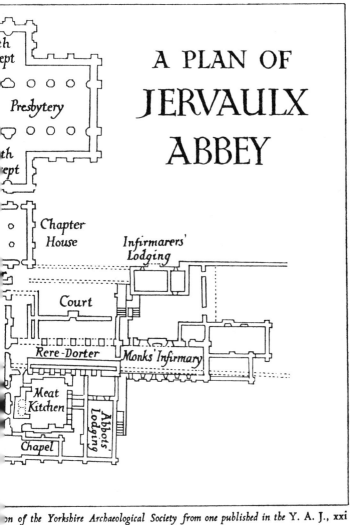

A PLAN OF

JERVAULX

ABBEY

h
ept

Presbytery

th
ept

Chapter
House

Infirmarers'
Lodging

Court

Rere-Dorter

Monks' Infirmary

Meat
Kitchen

Abbots' Lodging

Chapel

the Sunday procession in which they made a round of the buildings, sprinkling each with holy water. The chapter-house south of the south transept has a twelfth-century doorway, but is otherwise thirteenth century. Five octagonal piers, three with floriated capitals, remain of the arcades, and have, even without their arches, a look of grace. The nine grave slabs are mostly of abbots.

The lay brothers' quarters west of the cloister are the oldest part of the abbey, and are said to have been completed before the removal from Fors. Little remains of the monks' frater, but the wall of their dorter with its row of thirteenth-century lancets is the highest part of the ruins. Between these is the warming chamber where the monks warmed themselves when working in the cloisters, and the only place in the abbey which had a fire. South of this is the misericorde, where, after the middle of the fifteenth century, the monks could eat meat three days in the week, except during fasting seasons. The abbot's lodging was built in the fourteenth century when the first strict Cistercian rule that the abbot should eat and sleep with the rest of the community was relaxed; at this time a chapel for the use of the abbot was built. The kitchens with their three great fireplaces are fifteenth century. The infirmary had a small chapel and a detached kitchen. In most cases these remains are only foundations, but they are fascinating to trace, and to imagine from a little the whole. Standing yet in fields, they give an idea of the great extent of the abbey.

It was with dismay that the monks and the people of the district heard of the approaching dissolution of the monasteries. Two or three hundred people here joined the revolt against it, the Pilgrimage of Grace, and having gathered on the moors came down to Jervaulx to entreat Abbot Sedbergh to be on their side. He, realizing the hopelessness of the rebellion, slipped away to Witton Fell, taking with him a man and a boy, and telling his other servants to depart to their houses and save their goods and cattle. He remained on the fell four days, returning to the abbey at night. The rebels moved on to Richmond, but, hearing that the abbot had declared that no man who followed them should be his servant, they returned, and demanded that a new abbot should be elected. The brethren rang the chapel bell and prepared to choose a new abbot, but some refused to take part, and the rebels threatened to burn down the house. Then the brethren sent men to seek the abbot on the fell, and to save his house from burning he came back. The rebels tried to kill him, calling him a traitor, but at last they commanded him to take the oath and come with them; later he was allowed to return to Jervaulx. In 1537 he was hanged at Tyburn for participating in the rebellion, and the following year the abbey was destroyed.

A letter written in 1537 by Sir Arthur Darcy says: 'I was with my Lord Lieutenant at the suppression of Gervayes, which is wholly covered with lead, and there is one of the fairest churches I have ever seen, fair meadows, and the river running by it, and a great demesne.' In 1538 Richard Bellyseys wrote to his employer: 'I have taken down all the lead of Jervaulx— and as concerning the raising and taking down the house

—the ways in that country are so foul and deep that
no caryage can pass in wyntre—I am mynded to lett it
stand to the spring of the yere.' More letters show how
ruthless was the destruction; all that was of value was taken.

With Jervaulx the dale ends. There is no sudden
change; the rolling country between it and Ripon is
broken here and there by stretches of common, re-
minders of what is behind. Jervaulx belongs to the dale,
but for Fors it might never have been here. The monks
went, and their abbey walls fell, but their granges have
become farms; bridges which they built, churches they
owned, and industries they started, remain; and the
great stretch of Abbotside at the head of the dale bears
their name. They bind you through the generations to
those first dwellers on the hills. Standing in these
green meadows, you are still possessed by the calm and
strength of the fells. You realize again the completeness of the dale, so that a chance word bringing to
memory a part of it brings at the same time the whole.

INDEX

W E N S I

in the NORTH R

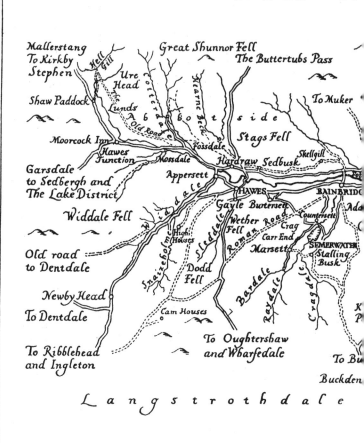

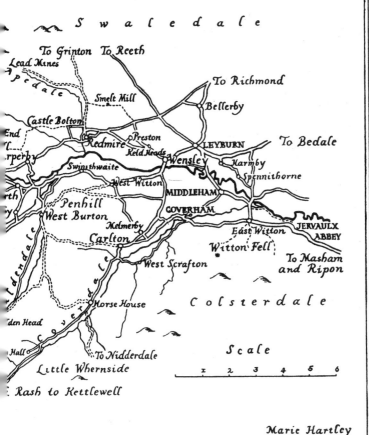

S w a l e d a l e

To Grinton   To Reeth

Lead Mines

pedale

To Richmond

Smelt Mill

Bellerby

Castle Bolton

End

Preston

rperby

Redmire

Keld Heads

LEYBURN

To Bedale

Swinithwaite

Wensley

Harmby

West Witton

Spennithorne

rth

MIDDLEHAM

y

Penhill

West Burton

COVERHAM

Melmerby

East Witton

JERVAULX
ABBEY

Carlton

Witton Fell

To Masham
and Ripon

West Scrafton

C o l s t e r d a l e

den Head

Horse House

Hall

To Nidderdale

S c a l e

Little Whernside

1   2   3   4   5   6

Rash to Kettlewell

Marie Hartley